AFTER HIS OWN HEART

"A Journey Through the Heart of the Psalms: Weekly Devotions to Inspire, Meditate, and Memorize"

Jeff Crosby

The Psalms

1. **Psalm 1** – Wisdom & Instruction – The way of the righteous and the way of the wicked.

2. **Psalm 2** – Messianic – The reign of the Lord's anointed.

3. **Psalm 3** – Lament & Trust – A cry for help and protection.

4. **Psalm 6** – Lament & Trust – A prayer in times of distress.

5. **Psalm 8** – Praise & Worship – God's glory in creation and our place in it.

6. **Psalm 9** – Thanksgiving & Remembrance – Praise for God's justice.

7. **Psalm 13** – Lament & Trust – A short lament, asking God for help.

8. **Psalm 15** – Wisdom & Instruction – Who may dwell in God's sanctuary.

9. **Psalm 18** – Thanksgiving & Remembrance – A song of deliverance and thanksgiving.

10. **Psalm 19** – Praise & Worship – The beauty of God's creation and His Word.

11. **Psalm 22** – Messianic – A foreshadowing of Christ's suffering and victory.

12. **Psalm 23** – Lament & Trust – The Lord as our Shepherd.

13. **Psalm 24** – *Praise & Worship – God's sovereignty and holiness.*
14. **Psalm 25** – *Wisdom & Instruction – A prayer for guidance and forgiveness.*
15. **Psalm 27** – *Lament & Trust – Confidence in God's protection.*
16. **Psalm 30** – *Thanksgiving & Remembrance – Thanksgiving for God's help.*
17. **Psalm 31** – *Lament & Trust – Trust in God during trouble.*
18. **Psalm 33** – *Praise & Worship – Praise for God's faithfulness and power.*
19. **Psalm 34** – *Thanksgiving & Remembrance – Thanking God for His deliverance.*
20. **Psalm 37** – *Wisdom & Instruction – Wisdom for the righteous in times of trouble.*
21. **Psalm 40** – *Thanksgiving & Remembrance – God's help and our response of praise.*
22. **Psalm 42** – *Lament & Trust – Longing for God in times of despair.*
23. **Psalm 46** – *Lament & Trust – God is our refuge and strength.*
24. **Psalm 47** – *Praise & Worship – God is King over all the earth.*
25. **Psalm 49** – *Wisdom & Instruction – The futility of trusting in wealth.*
26. **Psalm 51** – *Lament & Trust – A psalm of repentance.*
27. **Psalm 56** – *Lament & Trust – Trusting God when afraid.*
28. **Psalm 61** – *Lament & Trust – Crying out to God from a place of need.*

29. **Psalm 62** – *Lament & Trust – Finding rest and confidence in God.*

30. **Psalm 65** – *Praise & Worship – Praise for God's provision in nature.*

31. **Psalm 66** – *Thanksgiving & Remembrance – Remembering God's power and mercy.*

32. **Psalm 67** – *Praise & Worship – A prayer for God's blessing on the nations.*

33. **Psalm 69** – *Lament & Trust – A cry for salvation from enemies.*

34. **Psalm 73** – *Wisdom & Instruction – Struggling with the prosperity of the wicked.*

35. **Psalm 77** – *Lament & Trust – Remembering God's deeds in times of distress.*

36. **Psalm 86** – *Lament & Trust – A prayer for mercy and strength.*

37. **Psalm 91** – *Lament & Trust – God as our refuge and protection.*

38. **Psalm 92** – *Thanksgiving & Remembrance – A song for the Sabbath, praising God's deeds.*

39. **Psalm 96** – *Praise & Worship – Worship the Lord in the splendor of His holiness.*

40. **Psalm 100** – *Praise & Worship – A short psalm of thanksgiving.*

41. **Psalm 103** – *Praise & Worship – God's compassion and love for us.*

42. **Psalm 104** – *Praise & Worship – Praise for God's works in creation.*

43. **Psalm 111** – *Praise & Worship* – The greatness of God's works.

44. **Psalm 112** – *Wisdom & Instruction* – Blessings on those who fear the Lord.

45. **Psalm 113** – *Praise & Worship* – God lifts the needy and blesses His people.

46. **Psalm 118** – *Thanksgiving & Remembrance* – Gratitude for God's steadfast love.

47. **Psalm 119:9-16** – *Wisdom & Instruction* – On loving God's Word (just a portion of this longest psalm).

48. **Psalm 121** – *Lament & Trust* – Looking to God for help.

49. ***Psalm 130*** – *Lament & Trust* – *Waiting for the Lord's redemption.*

50. **Psalm 138** – *Praise & Worship* – Praise for answered prayer and God's steadfast love.

51. **Psalm 139** – *Lament & Trust* – God's intimate knowledge of us.

52. **Psalm 145** – *Praise & Worship* – Celebrating God's Greatness and Compassion

---

* All scripture quotations are from New Revised Standard Version Bible, copyright © 1989 National Council of the Churches of Christ in the United States of America. Used by permission. All rights reserved worldwide.

The Prologue

This book has been a passion project of mine, many years in the making. The concept has evolved a lot over time, and I have prayerfully considered how best to format it. What we have now started as a simple guide for going over a Psalm a week with friends and family—a guide that eventually developed into this full devotional book.

The Psalms offer us a unique glimpse into the heart of God from the hearts of those inspired by Him. We know that the Bible is the inspired Word of God, but the book of Psalms is especially unique because God reveals His character through the songs and prayers of the Psalmists. He uses their perspectives to connect with us in a powerful and relational way.

The chapters in Psalms vary between 2 verses and 176 verses. Some of the selected Psalms here are much longer than others. I wanted to preserve the Psalms as they were originally written and meant to be read, but feel free to break up each weekly devotional as you see fit. This isn't a race.

Each Psalm in this book includes a memorization guide. Don't feel pressured to memorize every word; this is a personal journey into the heart of God. Take your time. Memorize what you can but remember that everyone is in a unique place in their journey through Scripture.

Other verses are included with each Psalm to help you meditate on its message and themes. I have organized these hand-picked Psalms into several categories: Psalms of Praise & Worship, Psalms of Lament & Trust, Psalms of Thanksgiving & Remembrance, and even a few Messianic Psalms.

Each devotional also includes a quote from a well-known Christian author, pastor, or theologian, as well as a prayer. Feel free to personalize the prayer to your own life and circumstances.

My hope and prayer are that this devotional book will draw you closer to God through meditating on and even memorizing His Word.

Thank you for purchasing this book.

After HIS Own Heart

Walking in the Way of the Righteous

"Happy are those who do not follow the advice of the wicked, or take the path that sinners tread, or sit in the seat of scoffers; but their delight is in the law of the Lord, and on his law they meditate day and night. They are like trees planted by streams of water, which yield their fruit in its season, and their leaves do not wither. In all that they do, they prosper. The wicked are not so, but are like chaff that the wind drives away. Therefore the wicked will not stand in the judgment, nor sinners in the congregation of the righteous; for the Lord watches over the way of the righteous, but the way of the wicked will perish." – ***Psalm 1*** *(NRSV)*

Reflection:

Psalm 1 offers a beautiful description of two distinct paths: the way of the righteous and the way of the wicked. The psalm opens with a picture of the "happy" person—someone who resists the influence of wickedness and instead delights in God's Word. This delight is more than a casual interest; it's a deep, abiding joy in God's instruction, allowing His words to shape thoughts, actions, and desires.

Avoiding the Way of the Wicked

Psalm 1:1 describes the progression of sin: following, taking the path, and eventually sitting with those who oppose God's ways. This verse is a powerful reminder of the importance of choosing our influences wisely. Even small compromises can lead us into greater entanglements. Reflect on where you might need to distance yourself from influences or habits that draw you away from God's truth.

Related Verse: Proverbs 4:14-15 – "Do not enter the path of the wicked, and do not walk in the way of evildoers. Avoid it; do not go on it; turn away from it and pass on."

Delighting in God's Word

The psalmist describes the righteous person as someone who *delights* in God's law, meditating on it day and night. This love for God's Word provides guidance, wisdom, and spiritual nourishment. To delight in God's Word is to find joy in His truths and promises, allowing them to be a light to our path and a source of strength in all situations.

Related Verse: Joshua 1:8 – "This book of the law shall not depart out of your mouth; you shall meditate on it day and night, so that you may be careful to act in accordance with all that is written in it. For then you shall make your way prosperous, and then you shall be successful."

Like a Tree Planted by Streams of Water

The imagery of a "tree planted by streams of water" captures the essence of stability, growth, and fruitfulness that comes from a life deeply rooted in God. This tree doesn't struggle for water or wither in dry seasons; it thrives and produces fruit. When we are planted in God's Word, we become spiritually resilient, finding our source of strength in Him rather than in fleeting circumstances.

Related Verse: Jeremiah 17:7-8 – "Blessed are those who trust in the Lord, whose trust is the Lord. They shall be like a tree planted by water, sending out its roots by the stream. It shall not fear when heat comes, and its leaves shall stay green."

The Path of the Wicked

In contrast, the wicked are described as "chaff that the wind drives away." Chaff is lightweight and rootless, easily scattered by the slightest breeze. This image underscores the fragility and instability of a life that ignores God. Unlike the deeply rooted tree, the life without God is directionless and ultimately leads to destruction.

Related Verse: Proverbs 10:25 – "When the tempest passes, the wicked are no more, but the righteous are established forever."

The Lord Watches Over the Righteous

Psalm 1 concludes with a promise: "the Lord watches over the way of the righteous." God is deeply aware of our lives, guiding and protecting us as we follow His path. The promise of His watchful care is a reminder that walking in righteousness is not only about avoiding sin but about living in a relationship with a loving, attentive God.

Related Verse: Psalm 121:8 – "The Lord will keep your going out and your coming in from this time on and forevermore."

Quote:

"The Bible will keep you from sin, or sin will keep you from the Bible." - D.L. Moody

Application:

Take time today to consider which path you are on. Are there influences or habits that you need to release to fully delight in God's Word? Reflect on how God's Word can be a source of strength, guidance, and resilience in your life. Commit to reading and meditating on Scripture, allowing its truths to shape your path, keeping you rooted and fruitful.

Prayer:

Lord, thank You for offering a path that leads to blessing and life. Help me to delight in Your Word and meditate on it day and night. Strengthen my heart to resist the ways of the world and instead, root myself in Your truth. Let my life be like a tree planted by streams of water, bearing fruit that glorifies You. Watch over my path, Lord, and guide me in righteousness. Amen.

Memorization Guide:
Step 1: Break Down the Psalm into Sections

1. **Verses 1-2**: The character of the righteous person.
2. **Verses 3-4**: The comparison between the righteous and the wicked.
3. **Verses 5-6**: The ultimate destiny of each path.

Step 2: Memorize by Key Themes and Visualizations
Section 1: The Character of the Righteous Person (Verses 1-2)

- *Verse 1*: Blessed is the one who avoids evil.
- *Verse 2*: The blessed one delights in God's law.

Mnemonic Tips:

- Picture a person carefully **walking**, **standing**, and **sitting** (the three verbs) while **avoiding sinful ways**.
- Visualize a **joyful person reading** the Bible or reflecting, symbolizing "delight in the law."

Verses:

- "Happy are those who do not follow the advice of the wicked, or take the path that sinners tread, or sit in the seat of scoffers;"
- "but their delight is in the law of the LORD, and on his law they meditate day and night."

Section 2: Comparison of Righteous and Wicked (Verses 3-4)

- *Verse 3*: The righteous are like a **tree planted by streams of water**.
- *Verse 4*: The wicked are like **chaff blown by the wind**.

Mnemonic Tips:
- Picture a **tree** by a **flowing stream**, full of **green leaves and fruit**.
- Picture **chaff** (the lightweight husk) **blowing away** in the wind.

Verses:
- "They are like trees planted by streams of water, which yield their fruit in its season, and their leaves do not wither. In all that they do, they prosper."
- "The wicked are not so, but are like chaff that the wind drives away."

Section 3: The Destiny of Each Path (Verses 5-6)
- *Verse 5*: The **wicked cannot stand** in judgment.
- *Verse 6*: God **watches over** the righteous; the **wicked perish**.

Mnemonic Tips:
- Visualize **wicked people unable to stand before a judge**.
- Picture a **well-lit path** guided by God's presence vs. a path that **fades into darkness**.

Verses:
- "Therefore the wicked will not stand in the judgment, nor sinners in the congregation of the righteous;"
- "for the LORD watches over the way of the righteous, but the way of the wicked will perish."

Step 3: Repetition and Recitation
1. **Memorize one verse at a time** with imagery in mind, repeating until you're comfortable.
2. **Combine verses into sections** gradually.
3. **Recite the full psalm** daily, visualizing the themes.

Summary of Key Images
- **Blessed person** avoiding wicked ways.
- **Delight in the law** of the Lord.
- **Tree by water** vs. **Chaff in the wind**.
- **Path under God's care** vs. **Way of the wicked perishing**.

Psalm 2 – The Reign of the Lord's Anointed

"Why do the nations conspire, and the peoples plot in vain? The kings of the earth take their stand, and the rulers gather together against the Lord and against his Anointed, saying, 'Let us break their chains and throw off their fetters.' The One enthroned in heaven laughs; the Lord scoffs at them. He rebukes them in his anger and terrifies them in his wrath, saying, 'I have installed my king on Zion, my holy mountain.' I will proclaim the Lord's decree: He said to me, 'You are my Son; today I have become your Father. Ask me, and I will make the nations your inheritance, the ends of the earth your possession. You will break them with a rod of iron; you will dash them to pieces like pottery.' Therefore, you kings, be wise; be warned, you rulers of the earth. Serve the Lord with fear and celebrate his rule with trembling. Kiss his son, or he will be angry and your way will lead to your destruction, for his wrath can flare up in a moment. Blessed are all who take refuge in him." – Psalm 2 (NRSV)

Reflection:

Psalm 2 is a messianic psalm that prophesies the reign of God's anointed King, Jesus Christ, over the nations. It starts with a picture of the futile rebellion of earthly rulers against God's divine authority and highlights the establishment of God's chosen King. Ultimately, this psalm underscores that no power can thwart God's plan, and all must submit to His reign. The psalm is a call to acknowledge God's sovereignty and find refuge in His Anointed One, who brings justice and peace.

The Futility of Rebellion

The psalm opens with a picture of nations conspiring and rulers plotting against God's authority. Despite their attempts to overthrow God's rule, their efforts are futile. God laughs at the rebellion of earthly rulers because He knows their end. This reminds us that no matter how powerful human rulers seem, they cannot compare to the supreme authority of God. Reflect on how you might see the powers of this world and recognize that God's will will always prevail.

Related Verses:
- **Isaiah 40:23-24** – "He brings princes to naught and reduces the rulers of this world to nothing. No sooner are they planted, no sooner are they sown, no sooner do they take root in the ground, than he blows on them and they wither, and a whirlwind sweeps them away like chaff."
- **1 Corinthians 1:27-28** – "But God chose the foolish things of the world to shame the wise; God chose the weak things of the world to shame the strong."

God's Chosen King

God's decree establishes His King in Zion, saying to Him, "You are my Son." This is a prophetic declaration of Jesus Christ, whose reign is established by the Father. Through Christ, God will establish His kingdom on earth, and His justice will be absolute. This psalm not only points to the coronation of Christ as the eternal King but also calls us to acknowledge His lordship in our lives. Reflect on how you acknowledge the authority of Christ in your life and the world around you.

Related Verses:
- **Acts 13:33** – "This he has fulfilled to us, their children, by raising Jesus; as also it is written in the second Psalm, 'You are my Son; today I have begotten you.'"
- **Revelation 19:16** – "On his robe and on his thigh he has this name written: King of kings and Lord of lords."

The Call to Reverence and Submission

The psalm calls earthly rulers to "serve the Lord with fear" and to "kiss the Son." This act of reverence and submission symbolizes acknowledging God's authority and submitting to His sovereignty. For us, this is an invitation to submit to Christ, who is the King of all. Reflect on what it means for you to submit to God's rule and find refuge in the protection and peace that His reign offers.

Related Verses:
- **Philippians 2:10-11** – "That at the name of Jesus every knee should bow, in heaven and on earth and under the earth, and every tongue confess that Jesus Christ is Lord, to the glory of God the Father."
- **Psalm 110:1** – "The Lord says to my Lord: 'Sit at my right hand until I make your enemies your footstool.'"

Blessing in Submission

The psalm ends with a blessing for those who take refuge in God's Anointed. In Christ, there is protection, salvation, and peace. This psalm assures us that those who submit to God's plan and place their trust in His Anointed One will be blessed. Reflect on how you have found refuge in Christ and how that brings peace in a tumultuous world.

Related Verses:
- **Romans 8:1** – "There is therefore now no condemnation for those who are in Christ Jesus."
- **Psalm 5:11** – "But let all who take refuge in you rejoice; let them ever sing for joy, and spread your protection over them, that those who love your name may exult in you."

Quote:
"Jesus is not the King of a few people; He is the King of kings,

and He is coming back to rule the world." – Billy Graham

Application:
Reflect on how you respond to the authority of Christ. Do you recognize His sovereignty in every aspect of your life? This psalm calls us to bow before the King of kings, to serve Him with reverence, and to take refuge in His protection. Spend time today meditating on Christ's reign and how you can live in submission to His lordship.

Prayer:
Lord, thank You for sending Your Anointed One, Jesus Christ, to reign over all the earth. I acknowledge Your sovereignty and submit to Your rule in my life. Help me to take refuge in You, trusting in Your justice and peace. May I find joy and blessing in Your reign and live as one who honors and serves You with fear and trembling. Amen.

Memorization Guide:
Step 1: Break Down the Psalm into Sections
1. **Verses 1-3**: The rebellion of the nations.
2. **Verses 4-6**: God's sovereign response.
3. **Verses 7-9**: The proclamation of the King's authority.
4. **Verses 10-12**: The call to wisdom and reverence.

Step 2: Memorize by Key Themes and Visualizations
- **Section 1**: Nations conspiring in vain (visualize rulers plotting, but God laughing from heaven).
- **Section 2**: God's sovereign response (picture God on His throne, declaring His victory).

- **Section 3**: The King established (visualize Christ on the throne, reigning over all).
- **Section 4**: A call to honor God's rule (picture yourself bowing in submission and peace).

Verses:
- "Why do the nations conspire and the peoples plot in vain?"
- "I have installed my king on Zion, my holy mountain."
- "You are my Son; today I have become your Father."
- "Serve the Lord with fear and celebrate his rule with trembling."

Step 3: Repetition and Recitation
1. Memorize one section at a time.
2. Gradually combine the sections into the full psalm.
3. Recite the psalm daily, visualizing the key themes.

Summary of Key Images:
- Earthly rulers conspiring in vain.
- God's laughter and sovereignty.
- The anointed King reigning from Zion.
- A call to submit to God's authority and find refuge in Christ.

Psalm 3 – A Cry for Help and Protection

"O Lord, how many are my foes! Many are rising against me; many are saying to my soul, 'There is no help for you in God.' Selah. But you, O Lord, are a shield about me, my glory, and the lifter of my head. I cry aloud to the Lord, and he answers me from his holy hill. Selah. I lie down and sleep; I wake again, for the Lord sustains me. I am not afraid of ten thousands of people who have set themselves against me all around. Arise, O Lord! Save me, O my God! For you strike all my enemies on the cheek; you break the teeth of the wicked. Salvation belongs to the Lord; your blessing be on your people! Selah." – Psalm 3 (NRSV)

Reflection:
Psalm 3 is a prayer of lament, where David, surrounded by enemies, turns to God for protection and salvation. It emphasizes trust in God's ability to deliver, even in the face of overwhelming adversity. Despite the many threats around him, David finds peace in knowing that God is his shield and sustainer. This psalm encourages us to turn to God in times of trouble, trusting that He is our refuge and source of salvation.

Facing Our Foes
David begins by acknowledging the multitude of enemies who threaten him, yet his confidence remains in God's protection. In moments of crisis, it can feel like the world is against us, but this psalm reminds us that God is greater than any enemy. Reflect on any struggles or fears you may be facing, and consider how you can place your trust in God as your defender.

Related Verses:
- **Psalm 34:19** – "Many are the afflictions of the righteous, but the Lord delivers him out of them all."

- **Isaiah 41:10** – "Do not fear, for I am with you; do not be dismayed, for I am your God. I will strengthen you and help you; I will uphold you with my righteous right hand."

God is Our Shield and Glory

David declares, "But you, O Lord, are a shield about me, my glory, and the lifter of my head." In the face of opposition, God provides protection and honor. When we feel defeated or low, God is the one who lifts our heads, offering dignity and strength. Consider how God has been your shield and glory in past difficulties and thank Him for His constant protection.

Related Verses:
- **Psalm 28:7** – "The Lord is my strength and my shield; in him my heart trusts, and I am helped."
- **Psalm 18:2** – "The Lord is my rock, my fortress, and my deliverer; my God, my rock, in whom I take refuge."

Rest in God's Sustaining Power

David finds peace, even in the midst of danger, saying, "I lie down and sleep; I wake again, for the Lord sustains me." True rest comes when we trust that God is in control. No matter the threats or challenges, He is the one who sustains us. Reflect on how God has given you rest during times of stress, and how you can continue to rest in His faithfulness.

Related Verses:
- **Psalm 4:8** – "In peace I will both lie down and sleep; for you alone, O Lord, make me dwell in safety."
- **Matthew 11:28** – "Come to me, all you that are weary and are carrying heavy burdens, and I will give you rest."

Trusting in God's Salvation

The psalm ends with David proclaiming that salvation belongs to the Lord. This declaration of faith reinforces the truth that only God can deliver. As you face challenges in your life, remind yourself that ultimate victory and salvation rest in God alone. Reflect on the ways you have experienced God's deliverance and give thanks for His faithfulness.

Related Verses:
- **Isaiah 12:2** – "Behold, God is my salvation; I will trust, and will not be afraid; for the Lord God is my strength and my song, and he has become my salvation."
- **Psalm 62:1-2** – "For God alone my soul waits in silence; from him comes my salvation. He alone is my rock and my salvation, my fortress; I shall not be greatly shaken."

Quote:
"**Faith is the refusal to panic.**" – Martyn Lloyd-Jones

Application:
Take a moment to assess the "enemies" or challenges in your life. Are there areas where you need to trust God more deeply for protection and deliverance? Reflect on how you can rest in His sustaining power and walk in the confidence that He is your shield.

Prayer:
Lord, thank You for being my protector and sustainer. In times of fear and trouble, I trust in Your strength and provision. Help me to rest in Your care, knowing that You are always with me. Deliver me from all that threatens me, and let me find peace in Your presence. Amen.

After HIS Own Heart

Memorization Guide:

Step 1: Break Down the Psalm into Sections

1. **Verses 1-2**: The cry of distress.
2. **Verses 3-4**: God as shield and glory.
3. **Verses 5-6**: Trust in God's sustaining power.
4. **Verses 7-8**: Salvation belongs to God.

Step 2: Memorize by Key Themes and Visualizations

- **Section 1**: A cry for help amidst opposition (visualize being surrounded by threats).
- **Section 2**: God as shield and glory (visualize God as a protective force around you).
- **Section 3**: Resting in God's peace (picture lying down peacefully, knowing God sustains you).
- **Section 4**: Salvation belongs to God (visualize God's hand lifting you out of trouble).

Verses:

- "O Lord, how many are my foes! Many are rising against me."
- "But you, O Lord, are a shield about me, my glory, and the lifter of my head."
- "Salvation belongs to the Lord; your blessing be on your people!"

Step 3: Repetition and Recitation

1. Memorize one section at a time.
2. Gradually combine the sections into the full psalm.
3. Recite the psalm daily, visualizing the key themes.

Summary of Key Images:
- Oppressed by many foes.
- God as shield and glory.
- Resting in God's sustaining power.
- Salvation as God's gift.

Psalm 6 – A Prayer in Times of Distress

"O Lord, do not rebuke me in your anger, or discipline me in your wrath. Be gracious to me, O Lord, for I am languishing; heal me, O Lord, for my bones are troubled. My soul also is greatly troubled. But you, O Lord—how long? Turn, O Lord, deliver my life; save me for the sake of your steadfast love. For in death there is no remembrance of you; in Sheol who can give you praise? I am weary with my moaning; every night I flood my bed with tears; I drench my couch with my weeping. My eye wastes away because of grief; it grows weak because of all my foes. Depart from me, all you workers of evil, for the Lord has heard the sound of my weeping. The Lord has heard my supplication; the Lord accepts my prayer. All my enemies shall be ashamed and greatly troubled; they shall turn back and be put to shame in a moment." – Psalm 6 (NRSV)

Reflection:

Psalm 6 is a heartfelt prayer of lament. The psalmist is overwhelmed by physical, emotional, and spiritual distress and turns to God in complete dependence, pleading for mercy and healing. It is a raw expression of sorrow, but also a declaration of trust in God's steadfast love and His ability to deliver. This psalm teaches us to approach God honestly in times of trouble, to express our deepest pain, and to rest in His mercy and faithfulness.

A Cry for Mercy

The psalm opens with an earnest plea for God's mercy. The psalmist acknowledges that while God's discipline is just, he is overwhelmed and in need of grace. This plea for mercy is a reminder that in times of suffering, we can always approach God with humility, asking for His compassion. Reflect on your own struggles and how God's mercy has been evident in your life.

Related Verses:
- **Lamentations 3:22-23** – "The steadfast love of the Lord never ceases; his mercies never come to an end; they are new every morning; great is your faithfulness."
- **Psalm 51:1-2** – "Have mercy on me, O God, according to your steadfast love; according to your abundant mercy blot out my transgressions. Wash me thoroughly from my iniquity, and cleanse me from my sin."

Desperation and Trust in God's Steadfast Love

The psalmist's distress is evident in his description of weeping and physical exhaustion. But even in his deepest sorrow, he appeals to God's "steadfast love," trusting that God's love will bring deliverance. This contrast reminds us that while our circumstances may feel unbearable, God's love is constant and unwavering. Reflect on how you can rest in God's unfailing love during difficult times.

Related Verses:
- **Romans 8:38-39** – "For I am convinced that neither death nor life, neither angels nor demons, neither the present nor the future, nor any powers, neither height nor depth, nor anything else in all creation, will be able to separate us from the love of God that is in Christ Jesus our Lord."
- **Psalm 136:1** – "Give thanks to the Lord, for he is good. His love endures forever."

The Burden of Grief

The psalmist's tears have soaked his bed, and his grief has worn him down. The psalm vividly portrays the depth of emotional pain and anguish. This reminds us that it's okay to cry out to God and express our sorrow—He hears our weeping and cares deeply for us in our pain. Reflect on how God has been present in your times of grief and how He has comforted you.

Related Verses:

- **Psalm 56:8** – "You have kept count of my tossings; put my tears in your bottle. Are they not in your book?"

- **2 Corinthians 1:3-4** – "Praise be to the God and Father of our Lord Jesus Christ, the Father of compassion and the God of all comfort, who comforts us in all our troubles, so that we can comfort those in any trouble with the comfort we ourselves receive from God."

Confidence in God's Hearing and Answering Prayer

The psalmist declares, "The Lord has heard the sound of my weeping... He accepts my prayer." This assurance that God hears and answers prayer provides hope amidst suffering. We can be confident that God not only hears our cries but also answers according to His perfect timing. Reflect on the times God has answered your prayers, whether in moments of great joy or deep sorrow.

Related Verses:

- **1 John 5:14-15** – "This is the confidence we have in approaching God: that if we ask anything according to his will, he hears us. And if we know that he hears us—whatever we ask—we know that we have what we asked of him."

- **Psalm 34:17** – "The righteous cry out, and the Lord hears them; he delivers them from all their troubles."

Quote:

"God's mercy is greater than your sin, and His love is stronger

than your fears." – Max Lucado

Application:
Are there areas in your life where you are experiencing sorrow or distress? Like the psalmist, bring those struggles before God, knowing He hears your prayers. Take time to reflect on God's mercy and love in your life, and allow it to encourage you in your own times of grief. Even in your darkest moments, God's love remains steadfast and His deliverance is sure.

Prayer:
Lord, I come to You with my pain and sorrow, knowing that You hear me. In times of grief, I trust in Your steadfast love and mercy. I ask for Your healing, not just in my body but in my heart and soul. Thank You for Your compassion and for hearing my cries. Please strengthen me, comfort me, and help me to rest in Your faithfulness. Amen.

Memorization Guide:
Step 1: Break Down the Psalm into Sections
1. **Verses 1-2**: The cry for mercy.
2. **Verses 3-4**: The plea for deliverance based on God's love.
3. **Verses 5-7**: The expression of sorrow and grief.
4. **Verses 8-10**: Confidence in God's response to prayer.

Step 2: Memorize by Key Themes and Visualizations
- **Section 1**: Crying for mercy (visualize the psalmist calling out to God for grace).
- **Section 2**: Pleading for deliverance based on God's love (visualize a loving, merciful God).

- **Section 3**: Weeping in grief (visualize the psalmist's tears and deep sorrow).
- **Section 4**: Trusting God to hear and answer (visualize God listening and responding).

Verses:
- "O Lord, do not rebuke me in your anger, or discipline me in your wrath."
- "Be gracious to me, O Lord, for I am languishing; heal me, O Lord, for my bones are troubled."
- "The Lord has heard the sound of my weeping; the Lord accepts my prayer."
- "All my enemies shall be ashamed and greatly troubled."

Step 3: Repetition and Recitation
1. Memorize one section at a time.
2. Gradually combine the sections into the full psalm.
3. Recite the psalm daily, visualizing the key themes.

Summary of Key Images:
- A cry for mercy in distress.
- Pleading for deliverance based on God's love.
- Tears and sorrow as expressions of deep grief.
- Confidence that God hears and answers prayer.

Psalm 8 – God's Glory in Creation and Our Place in It

"O Lord, our Lord, how majestic is your name in all the earth! You have set your glory above the heavens. Out of the mouths of babes and infants, you have established strength because of your foes, to still the enemy and the avenger. When I look at your heavens, the work of your fingers, the moon and the stars, which you have set in place, what is man that you are mindful of him, and the son of man that you care for him? Yet you have made him a little lower than the heavenly beings and crowned him with glory and honor. You have given him dominion over the works of your hands; you have put all things under his feet, all sheep and oxen, and also the beasts of the field, the birds of the heavens, and the fish of the sea, whatever passes along the paths of the seas. O Lord, our Lord, how majestic is your name in all the earth!" – Psalm 8 (NRSV)

Reflection:

Psalm 8 is a beautiful meditation on the majesty of God's creation and the unique place of humanity within it. The psalmist begins and ends with a declaration of the greatness of God's name. In the midst of contemplating the vastness of the universe, the psalmist is struck by the fact that God, the Creator of all, is mindful of humanity and has entrusted us with dominion over creation. This psalm encourages us to awe in God's greatness, while also humbling us to recognize the responsibility He has given us.

The Majesty of God's Name

The psalm opens with a majestic declaration of God's name being revered across all of creation. The earth and heavens display His glory, and even the smallest beings—babies and infants—testify to His power and greatness. When we reflect on the vastness of the universe, we cannot help but be humbled by the fact that God's glory surpasses everything. Reflect on how you can better honor God's majestic name in your daily life.

Related Verses:
- **Psalm 19:1** – "The heavens declare the glory of God; the sky proclaims the work of his hands."
- **Isaiah 42:8** – "I am the Lord; that is my name; I will not yield my glory to another or my praise to idols."

God's Glory in Creation

The psalmist gazes upon the heavens, the moon, and the stars, marveling at the work of God's fingers. The vastness of the cosmos is a reflection of the greatness of its Creator. When we contemplate the natural world, we should be filled with awe at God's power and artistry. Take a moment to consider how the beauty of creation speaks to God's majesty. How can you spend more time reflecting on His greatness through the world around you?

Related Verses:
- **Genesis 1:1** – "In the beginning, God created the heavens and the earth."
- **Romans 1:20** – "For since the creation of the world, God's invisible qualities—his eternal power and divine nature—have been clearly seen, being understood from what has been made, so that people are without excuse."

Our Dignity and Responsibility

The psalmist asks, "What is man that you are mindful of him?" In the grand expanse of the universe, it seems unfathomable that God would care about humanity. Yet, God has made us "a little lower than the heavenly beings" and has crowned us with glory and honor. Despite our smallness in the grand scheme of creation, God has entrusted us with the responsibility of caring for the earth. This humbling reality should inspire us to steward creation with responsibility and reverence. Reflect on your own role in God's creation—how do you honor the responsibility He has given you to care for the earth?

Related Verses:

- **Genesis 1:26-28** – "Then God said, 'Let us make mankind in our image, in our likeness, so that they may rule over the fish in the sea and the birds in the sky, over the livestock and all the wild animals, and over all the creatures that move along the ground.'"

- **Psalm 115:16** – "The highest heavens belong to the Lord, but the earth he has given to mankind."

Dominion Over Creation

God has given humanity dominion over creation, a responsibility that comes with both privilege and stewardship. We are entrusted with the care of all living things, from animals to the environment. Reflect on how you use your influence and resources to care for the world around you. How can you live out this calling to steward creation well, reflecting God's image through your actions?

Related Verses:

- **Psalm 104:24** – "How many are your works, Lord! In wisdom you made them all; the earth is full of your creatures."

- **Matthew 25:21** – "His master replied, 'Well done, good and faithful servant! You have been faithful with a few things; I will put you in charge of many things. Come and share your master's happiness!'"

Quote:
"The more I see of the greatness of God, the more I feel the weight of His glory and my responsibility to reflect that greatness." – John Piper

Application:
Take time today to reflect on the greatness of God as revealed in His creation. How does contemplating the vastness of the universe or the intricacy of life around you draw you closer to Him? Consider the responsibility you've been given to care for creation and how you can live more faithfully as a steward of the earth.

Prayer:
Lord, how majestic is Your name in all the earth! As I look at the beauty and wonder of creation, I stand in awe of Your power and majesty. Thank You for entrusting me with the responsibility to care for the world You have made. Help me to live with a deeper reverence for You and to reflect Your glory through my stewardship of creation. May my life bring honor to Your name in all things. Amen.

Memorization Guide:
Step 1: Break Down the Psalm into Sections
1. **Verses 1-2:** The majesty of God's name.
2. **Verses 3-4:** Contemplation of the heavens and God's creation.
3. **Verses 5-8:** Our dignity and responsibility in creation.
4. **Verse 9:** Closing declaration of God's majesty.

Step 2: Memorize by Key Themes and Visualizations
- **Section 1**: God's majestic name (visualize the vastness of the earth and sky declaring His glory).
- **Section 2**: The beauty of the heavens (visualize the stars, moon, and sky reflecting God's craftsmanship).
- **Section 3**: Humanity's dignity and responsibility (picture yourself caring for animals and the earth as God's steward).
- **Section 4**: A closing reminder of God's majesty (visualize a world resounding with praise to God).

Verses:
- "O Lord, our Lord, how majestic is your name in all the earth!"
- "When I look at your heavens, the work of your fingers, the moon and the stars, which you have set in place."
- "What is man that you are mindful of him, and the son of man that you care for him?"
- "You have made him a little lower than the heavenly beings and crowned him with glory and honor."

Step 3: Repetition and Recitation
1. Memorize one section at a time.
2. Gradually combine the sections into the full psalm.
3. Recite the psalm daily, visualizing the key themes.

Summary of Key Images:
- The majestic name of God.

- The grandeur of creation reflecting God's glory.
- The dignity and responsibility of humanity in creation.
- God's sovereignty and our stewardship.

Psalm 9 – Praise for God's Justice

"I will give thanks to the Lord with my whole heart; I will tell of all your wonderful deeds. I will be glad and exult in you; I will sing praise to your name, O Most High. When my enemies turn back, they stumble and perish before you. For you have maintained my just cause; you have sat on the throne giving righteous judgment. You have rebuked the nations, you have destroyed the wicked; you have blotted out their name forever and ever. The enemy has come to an end in everlasting ruins; their cities you have rooted out; the very memory of them has perished. But the Lord sits enthroned forever; he has established his throne for justice, and he judges the world with righteousness; he judges the peoples with equity. The Lord is a stronghold for the oppressed, a stronghold in times of trouble. And those who know your name put their trust in you, for you, O Lord, have not forsaken those who seek you. Sing praises to the Lord, who dwells in Zion. Tell among the peoples his deeds. For he who avenges blood is mindful of them; he does not forget the cry of the afflicted. Be gracious to me, O Lord. See my affliction from those who hate me, O you who lift me up from the gates of death, that I may recount all your praises, that in the gates of the daughter of Zion I may rejoice in your salvation. The nations have sunk in the pit that they made; in the net that they hid, their own foot has been caught. The Lord has made himself known; he has executed judgment; the wicked are snared in the work of their own hands. The wicked shall return to Sheol, all the nations that forget God. For the needy shall not always be forgotten, and the hope of the poor shall not perish forever. Arise, O Lord! Let not man prevail; let the nations be judged before you. Put them in fear, O Lord! Let the nations know that they are but men." – Psalm 9 (NRSV)

Reflection:
Psalm 9 is a psalm of praise and thanksgiving for God's justice. The psalmist expresses gratitude for God's righteous rule and His care for the oppressed. The psalm speaks to God's judgment against the wicked and His protection of those who trust in Him. It is a call to recognize God as the righteous Judge of all the earth, who executes justice with fairness, while also being a refuge for the oppressed and downtrodden. This psalm encourages us to praise God for His justice and to trust that He will right all wrongs.

Thanksgiving for God's Justice
The psalm begins with the psalmist expressing his thanks to God for His wonderful deeds. There is a deep sense of gratitude for God's justice, which is a recurring theme in the psalm. The psalmist is confident that the Lord maintains His people's cause and protects them from their enemies. Reflect on the ways God has shown His justice in your life and how you can thank Him for His righteousness.

Related Verses:
- **Psalm 98:1** – "Oh sing to the Lord a new song, for he has done marvelous things! His right hand and his holy arm have worked salvation for him."

- **Psalm 34:17-18** – "When the righteous cry for help, the Lord hears and delivers them out of all their troubles. The Lord is near to the brokenhearted and saves the crushed in spirit."

The Lord's Righteous Judgment
The psalmist praises God for sitting on the throne and administering righteous judgment. God's rule is not only eternal

but just. He judges the world with righteousness, and no one can escape His justice. The wicked are brought low by their own actions, while God upholds the cause of the righteous. Reflect on God's perfect justice—how does it bring you comfort, knowing that He judges with equity and fairness?

Related Verses:
- **Psalm 96:13** – "Let all creation rejoice before the Lord, for he comes, he comes to judge the earth. He will judge the world in righteousness and the peoples in his faithfulness."
- **Romans 2:6** – "He will repay each person according to what they have done."

God's Refuge for the Oppressed

In the midst of His righteous judgment, God is also a stronghold for the oppressed, a refuge in times of trouble. The psalm reminds us that God is always present to defend and protect those who seek Him. No matter what struggles or afflictions we face, we can trust that God will not forsake us. Reflect on how God has been a refuge in your life, especially during times of trouble, and how you can find hope in His protection.

Related Verses:
- **Psalm 46:1** – "God is our refuge and strength, an ever-present help in trouble."
- **Psalm 25:16-17** – "Turn to me and be gracious to me, for I am lonely and afflicted. The troubles of my heart are enlarged; bring me out of my distresses."

God's Justice for the Oppressed

The psalm also emphasizes that God is mindful of the cry of the afflicted. He does not forget those who suffer or the blood of the innocent. While the wicked may seem to prosper temporarily, God will bring them to justice. For those who are oppressed and forgotten by society, there is hope in God's ultimate justice. Reflect on how you can bring justice and mercy to the marginalized in your own community, knowing that God's justice will prevail in the end.

Related Verses:
- **Isaiah 61:8** – "For I, the Lord, love justice; I hate robbery and wrong. I will faithfully give them their recompense, and I will make an everlasting covenant with them."
- **Luke 18:7-8** – "And will not God give justice to his elect, who cry to him day and night? Will he delay long over them? I tell you, he will give justice to them speedily."

Quote:
"The greatest thing in the world is to know that you are loved by God and that His justice is on your side." – A.W. Tozer

Application:
Reflect on the justice of God and how it brings both comfort and accountability. God's justice means that all wrongs will be righted, and those who suffer will be vindicated. Praise God for His righteousness and trust in His ultimate judgment. Consider how you can seek justice in your community and how you can be a voice for those who are oppressed and marginalized.

Prayer:
Lord, thank You for Your perfect justice. I praise You for sitting on Your throne, ruling with righteousness and equity. I trust that You will right all wrongs and bring justice to those who are oppressed. Help me to seek justice in my own life and in the lives of those around me. I find refuge in You, Lord, and I thank You for being a

stronghold in times of trouble. Amen.

Memorization Guide:

Step 1: Break Down the Psalm into Sections

1. **Verses 1-2**: Thanksgiving for God's wonderful deeds.

2. **Verses 3-6**: The Lord's righteous judgment.

3. **Verses 7-10**: God as a refuge for the oppressed.

4. **Verses 11-20**: God's justice for the afflicted and the nations.

Step 2: Memorize by Key Themes and Visualizations

- **Section 1**: Thanking God for His marvelous deeds (visualize giving thanks to God with your whole heart).

- **Section 2**: God's righteous rule (picture God seated on His throne, judging with equity).

- **Section 3**: God as a refuge (visualize God as a strong tower, sheltering those in need).

- **Section 4**: God's ultimate justice (visualize God executing justice, the wicked falling, and the oppressed rejoicing).

Verses:

- "I will give thanks to the Lord with my whole heart; I will tell of all your wonderful deeds."

- "But the Lord sits enthroned forever; he has established his throne for justice."

- "The Lord is a stronghold for the oppressed, a stronghold in times of trouble."

- "Sing praises to the Lord, who dwells in Zion. Tell among the peoples his deeds."

Step 3: Repetition and Recitation
1. Memorize one section at a time.
2. Gradually combine the sections into the full psalm.
3. Recite the psalm daily, visualizing the key themes.

Summary of Key Images:
- Giving thanks for God's justice.
- God as a righteous judge seated on His throne.
- God as a refuge for the oppressed.
- The ultimate justice of God for all nations.

Psalm 13 – A Short Lament, Asking God for Help

"How long, O Lord? Will you forget me forever? How long will you hide your face from me? How long must I bear pain in my soul and have sorrow in my heart all day long? How long shall my enemy be exalted over me? Consider and answer me, O Lord my God! Give light to my eyes, or I will sleep the sleep of death, and my enemy will say, 'I have prevailed.' My foes will rejoice because I am shaken. But I trusted in your steadfast love; my heart shall rejoice in your salvation. I will sing to the Lord, because he has dealt bountifully with me." – Psalm 13 (NRSV)

Reflection:
Psalm 13 is a lament, expressing deep sorrow and a cry for help from a place of despair. The psalmist feels abandoned by God, pleading for His intervention in the midst of suffering. Despite the intense emotions of doubt and anguish, the psalmist ends on a note of trust and praise. This psalm encourages us to be honest with God in our struggles, expressing our pain while remembering that God's love and salvation are unwavering.

A Cry for Help
The psalm begins with the psalmist crying out, asking how long God will hide His face and leave him in pain. This raw expression of grief and confusion reflects the heart of someone who feels distant from God and overwhelmed by circumstances. It's a reminder that it's okay to express our pain and frustration before God. Reflect on a time when you've felt this way and consider how you can bring those feelings to God with honesty, trusting that He hears you.

Related Verses:

- **Psalm 42:9-10** – "I say to God, my rock, 'Why have you forgotten me? Why must I go about mourning, oppressed by the enemy?'"
- **Lamentations 3:20-21** – "My soul is downcast within me; yet this I call to mind and therefore I have hope."

God, Give Light to My Eyes

The psalmist pleads for God to "give light to my eyes," a metaphor for restoring hope and strength. In the midst of darkness, the psalmist asks for clarity and a renewal of spiritual vision. When we are in despair, it can feel like everything around us is shrouded in darkness, but God is the one who can bring light into our lives, even in the deepest moments of trouble. Reflect on how God has brought light into your life during times of despair, and trust that He will do so again.

Related Verses:

- **Psalm 18:28** – "For it is you who light my lamp; the Lord my God lightens my darkness."
- **2 Corinthians 4:6** – "For God, who said, 'Let light shine out of darkness,' has shone in our hearts to give the light of the knowledge of the glory of God in the face of Jesus Christ."

Trust in God's Steadfast Love

Despite the psalmist's doubts, he declares his trust in God's "steadfast love." The psalmist chooses to anchor his heart in the unchanging love of God, even when circumstances suggest otherwise. This is an act of faith—choosing to trust in God's love when it feels like we've been forgotten. Reflect on how you can cultivate this same trust in God's love in the midst of hardship, knowing that His love is steadfast and never fails.

Related Verses:

- **Romans 8:38-39** – "For I am convinced that neither death nor life, neither angels nor demons, neither the present nor the future, nor any powers, neither height nor depth, nor anything else in all creation, will be able to separate us from the love of God that is in Christ Jesus our Lord."
- **Psalm 33:22** – "Let your steadfast love, O Lord, be upon us, even as we hope in you."

Rejoicing in God's Salvation

The psalmist ends with a statement of hope: "my heart shall rejoice in your salvation." Even though the psalmist is in the midst of pain, he declares that his heart will ultimately rejoice in God's deliverance. This is a reminder that, no matter the current circumstances, we have a reason to hope because God will deliver us. Reflect on how God has delivered you in the past and take comfort in the knowledge that He will continue to work in your life, even when things seem bleak.

Related Verses:

- **Isaiah 12:2** – "Surely God is my salvation; I will trust and not be afraid. The Lord, the Lord himself, is my strength and my defense; he has become my salvation."
- **Habakkuk 3:18** – "Yet I will rejoice in the Lord; I will be joyful in God my Savior."

Quote:
"God is not only present in our joy but also in our sorrow. His faithfulness is not dependent on our circumstances, but on His unchanging nature." – Jerry Bridges

Application:
Reflect on your own experiences of pain or confusion. How can

you, like the psalmist, express your struggles honestly to God, but also choose to trust in His love and salvation? Consider the ways God has been faithful to you in the past and allow that to fuel your hope in the midst of current struggles. Make it a practice to praise God even in the midst of your darkest moments.

Prayer:
Lord, I come to You with my sorrow and my confusion, knowing that You are with me even when I can't see Your presence. Help me to trust in Your steadfast love, even when my circumstances seem overwhelming. Give light to my eyes and renew my hope in Your salvation. I rejoice in Your goodness, knowing that You are faithful to deliver me. Amen.

Memorization Guide:
Step 1: Break Down the Psalm into Sections
1. **Verses 1-2**: The cry for help and feeling abandoned.
2. **Verses 3-4**: Asking God to intervene and restore hope.
3. **Verses 5-6**: Trust in God's love and rejoicing in His salvation.

Step 2: Memorize by Key Themes and Visualizations
- **Section 1**: A cry for help (visualize calling out to God in the midst of darkness).
- **Section 2**: Asking for light and renewal (visualize God shining light into a dark room).
- **Section 3**: Trust and rejoicing in God's salvation (visualize resting in God's love and celebrating His deliverance).

Verses:
- "How long, O Lord? Will you forget me forever?"

- "Consider and answer me, O Lord my God! Give light to my eyes, or I will sleep the sleep of death."
- "But I trusted in your steadfast love; my heart shall rejoice in your salvation."
- "I will sing to the Lord, because he has dealt bountifully with me."

Step 3: Repetition and Recitation
1. Memorize one section at a time.
2. Gradually combine the sections into the full psalm.
3. Recite the psalm daily, visualizing the key themes.

Summary of Key Images:
- A cry for help in the midst of pain.
- Asking God for renewal and light.
- Trusting in God's love and celebrating His salvation.

Psalm 15 – Who May Dwell in God's Sanctuary?

"O Lord, who may abide in your tent? Who may dwell on your holy hill? Those who walk blamelessly and do what is right and speak the truth from their heart; who do not slander with their tongue and do no evil to their neighbor, nor take up a reproach against their friend; in whose eyes the wicked are despised, but who honor those who fear the Lord; who stand by their oath even to their hurt; who do not lend money at interest, and do not take a bribe against the innocent. Those who do these things shall never be moved."
– Psalm 15 (NRSV)

Reflection:
Psalm 15 presents a list of qualities that describe the kind of person who can dwell in God's presence. It focuses on righteousness, integrity, truthfulness, and a heart that honors others. The psalmist asks, "Who may abide in your tent?"—a question that speaks to the desire for intimacy with God. The answer is clear: those who live with moral integrity and walk in alignment with God's standards. This psalm challenges us to examine our hearts and lives, encouraging us to pursue holiness and righteousness as we seek to draw closer to God.

The Desire for God's Presence
The psalm begins with a profound question: "Who may dwell on your holy hill?" The psalmist is expressing a desire to be in God's presence, a longing to experience intimacy with the Creator. For the psalmist, to be in God's presence is the greatest privilege. Reflect on your own desire to dwell with God. Do you hunger for His presence and the holiness that comes with being close to Him?

Related Verses:

- **Psalm 27:4** – "One thing I asked of the Lord, that will I seek after: that I may dwell in the house of the Lord all the days of my life, to gaze upon the beauty of the Lord and to inquire in his temple."

- **Psalm 84:10** – "For a day in your courts is better than a thousand elsewhere. I would rather be a doorkeeper in the house of my God than dwell in the tents of wickedness."

Characteristics of the Righteous

The psalmist outlines specific behaviors that describe the righteous person who may dwell in God's presence:

- **Blamelessness** and **righteous living**: This speaks to living with integrity, doing what is right in God's eyes.

- **Truthfulness from the heart**: Honesty and transparency should be at the core of who we are.

- **Non-slander** and **good deeds toward others**: The righteous person does not speak ill of others but seeks to uplift and help.

- **Honoring those who fear the Lord**: Those who honor God are also to honor others who revere Him.

- **Faithfulness**: The righteous person keeps their word, even when it's difficult.

Reflect on how you measure up to these qualities. Are there areas where God is calling you to grow in holiness, integrity, or faithfulness?

Related Verses:

- **Proverbs 12:22** – "Lying lips are an abomination to the Lord, but those who act faithfully are his delight."

- **Matthew 5:37** – "Let what you say be simply 'Yes' or 'No'; anything more than this comes from evil."

Integrity and Honesty in Action

The psalm also speaks about the importance of standing by one's word, even when it causes personal harm, and not exploiting others for personal gain. This includes not lending money with interest or taking bribes against the innocent. God desires His people to live justly, honoring others and caring for their well-being above personal gain. Reflect on how you can honor others with your words, actions, and commitments.

Related Verses:

- **Luke 6:31** – "And as you wish that others would do to you, do so to them."
- **Proverbs 11:1** – "A false balance is an abomination to the Lord, but a just weight is his delight."

The Stability of the Righteous

The psalm ends with a powerful promise: "Those who do these things shall never be moved." The righteous person who lives according to God's standards will find stability, peace, and security in His presence. This is a profound promise that our lives will be rooted in God's faithfulness and will not be shaken by the storms of life. Reflect on how you can build your life on the foundation of God's truth, seeking His guidance and living in His presence.

Related Verses:

- **Psalm 16:8** – "I have set the Lord always before me; because he is at my right hand, I shall not be shaken."

- **Matthew 7:24-25** – "Everyone then who hears these words of mine and does them will be like a wise man who built his house on the rock. And the rain fell, and the floods came, and the winds blew and beat on that house, but it did not fall, because it had been founded on the rock."

Quote:
"Holiness is not a call to isolation from the world, but a call to be different from it, to live a life set apart for God, reflecting His character in everything we do." – Francis Chan

Application:
Take time today to reflect on the qualities outlined in Psalm 15. How do your actions and words reflect a heart that desires God's presence? Are there areas of your life where God is calling you to live with more integrity, truthfulness, and honor? Spend time in prayer asking God to help you live according to His righteous standards and to dwell in His presence with a pure heart.

Prayer:
Lord, thank You for the privilege of being able to draw near to You. Help me to walk in a way that honors You, with blamelessness, truth, and integrity. Show me where I need to grow in honoring others, being faithful to my word, and living justly. May my life reflect Your holiness, and may I dwell in Your presence forever. Amen.

Memorization Guide:
Step 1: Break Down the Psalm into Sections

1. **Verses 1-2**: The question of who can dwell in God's presence.
2. **Verses 3-5**: The qualities of the righteous.
3. **Verse 6**: The promise of stability for those who live righteously.

Step 2: Memorize by Key Themes and Visualizations
- **Section 1**: The longing for God's presence (visualize standing in God's holy place).
- **Section 2**: The characteristics of the righteous (visualize a person living with integrity, honoring others).
- **Section 3**: The promise of stability (visualize a tree planted firmly, unshaken by storms).

Verses:
- "O Lord, who may abide in your tent? Who may dwell on your holy hill?"
- "Those who walk blamelessly and do what is right and speak the truth from their heart."
- "Those who do these things shall never be moved."

Step 3: Repetition and Recitation
1. Memorize one section at a time.
2. Gradually combine the sections into the full psalm.
3. Recite the psalm daily, visualizing the key themes.

Summary of Key Images:
- Desire to dwell in God's holy place.
- Walking with integrity and truthfulness.

- Stability and security in God's presence.

Psalm 18 – A Song of Deliverance and Thanksgiving

"I love you, O Lord, my strength. The Lord is my rock and my fortress and my deliverer, my God, my rock, in whom I take refuge, my shield, and the horn of my salvation, my stronghold. I call upon the Lord, who is worthy to be praised, and I am saved from my enemies. The cords of death encompassed me; the torrents of destruction assailed me; the cords of Sheol entangled me; the snares of death confronted me. In my distress I called upon the Lord; to my God I cried for help. From his temple he heard my voice, and my cry to him reached his ears. Then the earth reeled and rocked; the mountains quaked and were shaken, because he was angry. Smoke went up from his nostrils and devouring fire from his mouth; glowing coals flamed forth from him. He bowed the heavens and came down; thick darkness was under his feet. He rode on a cherub and flew; he came swiftly on the wings of the wind. He made darkness his covering, his canopy around him, thick clouds, a gathering of water. Out of the brightness before him hailstones and coals of fire broke through his clouds. The Lord also thundered in the heavens, and the Most High uttered his voice, hailstones and coals of fire. And he sent out his arrows and scattered them; he flashed forth lightning and routed them. Then the channels of the sea were seen, and the foundations of the world were laid bare at your rebuke, O Lord, at the blast of the breath of your nostrils." – Psalm 18:1-15 (NRSV)

Reflection:

Psalm 18 is a powerful song of praise and thanksgiving from David, recounting how God delivered him from his enemies. The psalmist describes God as his refuge, strength, and deliverer, giving vivid images of God's power and majesty in delivering His people. The psalmist's heartfelt gratitude stems from a deep awareness of God's greatness and His saving acts in times of distress. This psalm calls us to remember and praise God for His faithful deliverance in our lives, encouraging us to call upon Him in times of trouble.

God as Our Strength and Refuge

The psalm begins with an expression of love for God, declaring Him as David's strength, rock, and refuge. These images symbolize God's stability and protection. When life feels uncertain, we can find comfort in knowing that God is a solid foundation, unwavering and faithful. Reflect on the ways God has been a refuge in your life. How has He been your "rock" in times of trouble?

Related Verses:

- **Psalm 62:2** – "He alone is my rock and my salvation, my fortress; I shall not be greatly shaken."
- **Isaiah 26:4** – "Trust in the Lord forever, for the Lord God is an everlasting rock."

God Hears Our Cry for Help

David recounts the moment when he was overwhelmed by danger and death. In his distress, he called out to God, and the Lord responded with great power. God's response was not passive; it was a mighty intervention, shaking the earth and sending out His arrows to defeat David's enemies. God hears our cries for help, and He is active in delivering His people. Reflect on times when you called out to God in desperation and experienced His faithful answer.

Related Verses:

- **Psalm 34:17** – "When the righteous cry for help, the Lord hears and delivers them out of all their troubles."

- **Exodus 2:23-25** – "During that long period, the king of Egypt died, and the Israelites groaned in their slavery and cried out, and their cry for help because of their slavery went up to God. God heard their groaning and remembered his covenant with Abraham, with Isaac and with Jacob."

The Majesty of God's Deliverance

The psalmist describes God's dramatic intervention with images of shaking earth, thunder, lightning, and fire. These mighty displays of power demonstrate God's sovereignty over the natural world and His ability to act on behalf of His people. When God steps into our lives, He moves with authority and might. Reflect on how you have witnessed God's power in your life, whether through spiritual victories, physical healings, or personal breakthroughs.

Related Verses:

- **Nahum 1:3** – "The Lord is slow to anger but great in power; the Lord will not leave the guilty unpunished. His way is in the whirlwind and the storm, and the clouds are the dust of his feet."

- **Psalm 29:3-4** – "The voice of the Lord is over the waters; the God of glory thunders, the Lord, thunders over the mighty waters. The voice of the Lord is powerful; the voice of the Lord is majestic."

God's Presence Brings Deliverance

The vivid descriptions of God's arrival—riding on a cherub and sending fire and lightning—convey the power and majesty of God's presence. When God steps into our situation, nothing can stand against Him. His presence brings ultimate deliverance and peace. Reflect on how you've experienced God's presence in your life, particularly in times when you felt overwhelmed or powerless.

Related Verses:
- **Psalm 18:28** – "For it is you who light my lamp; the Lord my God lightens my darkness."
- **Psalm 46:1** – "God is our refuge and strength, a very present help in trouble."

Quote:
"God's power is not a mere concept or theory; it is an active force in our lives, a strength that we can rely on in times of need." – Tony Evans

Application:
Reflect on God's power and majesty as described in this psalm. How can you apply this understanding of God's active presence in your own life? Take time to recall times when God has delivered you, and thank Him for His faithfulness. Consider how you can actively seek His presence and trust in His strength during challenges.

Prayer:
Lord, You are my rock, my fortress, and my deliverer. I praise You for Your mighty power and Your faithful response when I call on You. Thank You for being my refuge and for intervening in my life with strength and authority. Help me to remember Your past deliverances and trust in Your ability to deliver me now. May I always find security in Your presence, knowing that You are faithful and mighty to save. Amen.

Memorization Guide:

Step 1: Break Down the Psalm into Sections

1. **Verses 1-3**: A declaration of love for God as the source of strength and refuge.

2. **Verses 4-6**: Crying out to God in distress and His response.

3. **Verses 7-15**: The dramatic and mighty intervention of God.

Step 2: Memorize by Key Themes and Visualizations

- **Section 1**: God as our refuge (visualize standing firm on a rock in the midst of a storm).

- **Section 2**: Calling out to God in distress (visualize lifting up your voice to God, knowing He hears you).

- **Section 3**: God's mighty deliverance (visualize God stepping into your situation with power, shaking the earth and sending fire).

Verses:

- "I love you, O Lord, my strength. The Lord is my rock and my fortress and my deliverer."

- "In my distress I called upon the Lord; to my God I cried for help."

- "He bowed the heavens and came down; thick darkness was under his feet."

- "The Lord has made himself known; he has executed judgment."

Step 3: Repetition and Recitation
1. Memorize one section at a time.

2. Gradually combine the sections into the full psalm.

3. Recite the psalm daily, visualizing the key themes.

Summary of Key Images:
- God as the rock and refuge in times of trouble.
- Crying out to God and experiencing His mighty intervention.
- The dramatic display of God's power in delivering His people.

Psalm 19 – The Beauty of God's Creation and His Word

"The heavens declare the glory of God; the sky above proclaims his handiwork. Day to day pours out speech, and night to night reveals knowledge. There is no speech, nor are there words, whose voice is not heard. Their voice goes out through all the earth, and their words to the end of the world. In them he has set a tent for the sun, which comes out like a bridegroom leaving his chamber, and, like a strong man, runs its course with joy. Its rising is from the end of the heavens, and its circuit to the end of them, and there is nothing hidden from its heat. The law of the Lord is perfect, reviving the soul; the testimony of the Lord is sure, making wise the simple; the precepts of the Lord are right, rejoicing the heart; the commandment of the Lord is pure, enlightening the eyes; the fear of the Lord is clean, enduring forever; the rules of the Lord are true and righteous altogether. More to be desired are they than gold, even much fine gold; sweeter also than honey and drippings of the honeycomb. Moreover, by them is your servant warned; in keeping them there is great reward. Who can discern his errors? Declare me innocent from hidden faults. Keep back your servant also from presumptuous sins; let them not have dominion over me! Then I shall be blameless, and innocent of great transgression. Let the words of my mouth and the meditation of my heart be acceptable in your sight, O Lord, my rock and my redeemer." – Psalm 19 (NRSV)

Reflection:

Psalm 19 begins by highlighting the beauty of God's creation, particularly the heavens, which declare His glory. The vastness and intricacy of the natural world point us to the Creator and reveal His greatness. But the psalm doesn't stop there; it moves from the grandeur of creation to the perfection and power of God's Word. Both creation and Scripture speak to the greatness of God, guiding and instructing us toward wisdom, purity, and righteousness. This psalm invites us to consider how we respond to both the revelation of God through creation and His Word.

The Glory of God in Creation

The psalmist begins by observing how the heavens declare the glory of God. Every part of creation, from the vastness of the sky to the rhythm of the sun's movement, proclaims God's handiwork. The beauty and order in nature point us to a Creator who is powerful, wise, and intentional. Reflect on the beauty of creation and how it leads you to worship God. How does the natural world around you inspire awe in your heart for the Creator?

Related Verses:

- **Psalm 8:3-4** – "When I look at your heavens, the work of your fingers, the moon and the stars, which you have set in place, what is man that you are mindful of him, and the son of man that you care for him?"

- **Romans 1:20** – "For his invisible attributes, namely, his eternal power and divine nature, have been clearly perceived, ever since the creation of the world, in the things that have been made."

The Power of God's Word

Moving from creation, the psalmist shifts to describing the perfect nature of God's Word. The law of the Lord revives the soul and brings wisdom, joy, and understanding. God's commands are pure and righteous, and they are more valuable than gold and sweeter than honey. Reflect on the importance of God's Word in your life. How has the Bible revived your soul, brought joy to your heart, and guided you in wisdom? Do you treasure His Word above all else?

Related Verses:
- **2 Timothy 3:16-17** – "All Scripture is breathed out by God and profitable for teaching, for reproof, for correction, and for training in righteousness, that the man of God may be complete, equipped for every good work."
- **Proverbs 2:6** – "For the Lord gives wisdom; from his mouth come knowledge and understanding."

The Value of God's Word

The psalmist describes God's commandments as more desirable than gold, even much fine gold. They are sweeter than honey, providing us with more joy and satisfaction than the material treasures of this world. How often do you prioritize God's Word in your life over the pursuit of worldly treasures? Reflect on how God's Word satisfies the deepest longings of your heart in a way that nothing else can.

Related Verses:
- **Matthew 4:4** – "Man shall not live by bread alone, but by every word that comes from the mouth of God."
- **Psalm 119:72** – "The law of your mouth is better to me than thousands of gold and silver pieces."

God's Word and Its Transforming Power

The psalmist also acknowledges that through God's Word, we are warned, and by keeping it, there is great reward. But the psalmist goes further, asking God to cleanse him from hidden faults and to keep him from willful sins. The transformative power of God's Word leads us to a life of purity, wisdom, and righteousness. Reflect on how God's Word has revealed areas of your life that need transformation. Are there any hidden faults or areas of sin that God is asking you to surrender to Him?

Related Verses:
- **James 1:22** – "But be doers of the word, and not hearers only, deceiving yourselves."
- **Psalm 119:11** – "I have stored up your word in my heart, that I might not sin against you."

Quote:
"The Word of God is the most powerful agent of change in our lives, bringing us to a deeper understanding of who God is and who we are in Him." – Charles Stanley

Application:
Take time to meditate on both God's creation and His Word. Do you see how both reveal His glory and character? Reflect on how you can treasure God's Word more deeply in your life. How can you allow Scripture to transform your heart and mind, bringing you closer to God? Consider making God's Word a greater priority in your daily routine and let it shape your actions, decisions, and relationships.

Prayer:
Lord, thank You for the beauty of creation, which reveals Your glory and power. Thank You also for the gift of Your Word, which is perfect, pure, and life-giving. Help me to treasure Your Word above all else, to seek wisdom and guidance from it, and to allow it to transform my heart and mind. May Your Word lead me to greater intimacy with You

and greater righteousness in my life. Amen.

Memorization Guide:
Step 1: Break Down the Psalm into Sections
1. **Verses 1-6**: The glory of God in creation.
2. **Verses 7-11**: The perfection of God's Word.
3. **Verses 12-14**: A prayer for cleansing and purity.

Step 2: Memorize by Key Themes and Visualizations
- **Section 1**: Creation declaring God's glory (visualize the heavens and the earth proclaiming God's greatness).
- **Section 2**: The power and sweetness of God's Word (visualize treasure, like gold and honey, representing the value of Scripture).
- **Section 3**: A prayer for transformation (visualize God's Word cleansing and purifying your heart).

Verses:
- "The heavens declare the glory of God; the sky above proclaims his handiwork."
- "The law of the Lord is perfect, reviving the soul; the testimony of the Lord is sure, making wise the simple."
- "More to be desired are they than gold, even much fine gold; sweeter also than honey and drippings of the honeycomb."
- "Let the words of my mouth and the meditation of my heart be acceptable in your sight, O Lord, my rock and my redeemer."

Step 3: Repetition and Recitation

1. Memorize one section at a time.
2. Gradually combine the sections into the full psalm.
3. Recite the psalm daily, visualizing the key themes.

Summary of Key Images:
- Creation as a reflection of God's glory.
- The sweetness and value of God's Word.
- A prayer for cleansing and transformation.

Psalm 22 – A Cry of Suffering and Hope

"My God, my God, why have you forsaken me? Why are you so far from helping me, from the words of my groaning? O my God, I cry by day, but you do not answer; and by night, but find no rest. Yet you are holy, enthroned on the praises of Israel. In you our ancestors trusted; they trusted, and you delivered them. To you they cried and were saved; in you they trusted and were not put to shame. But I am a worm, and not human; scorned by others, and despised by the people. All who see me mock at me; they make mouths at me, they shake their heads; 'Commit your cause to the Lord; let him deliver—let him rescue the one in whom he delights!' Yet it was you who took me from the womb; you kept me safe on my mother's breast. On you I was cast from my birth, and since my mother bore me you have been my God. Do not be far from me, for trouble is near and there is no one to help. Many bulls encircle me, strong bulls of Bashan surround me; they open wide their mouths at me, like a ravening and roaring lion. I am poured out like water, and all my bones are out of joint; my heart is like wax; it is melted within my breast; my mouth is dried up like a potsherd, and my tongue sticks to my jaws; you lay me in the dust of death. For dogs are all around me; a company of evildoers encircles me; my hands and feet have shriveled; I can count all my bones. They stare and gloat over me; they divide my clothes among themselves, and for my clothing they cast lots. But you, O Lord, do not be far away! O my help, come quickly to my aid! Deliver my soul from the sword, my life from the power of the dog! Save me from the mouth of the lion! From the horns of the wild oxen you have rescued me. I will tell of your name to my brothers and sisters; in the midst of the congregation I will praise you: You who fear the Lord, praise him! All you offspring of Jacob, glorify him; stand in awe of him, all you offspring of Israel! For he did not despise or abhor the affliction of the afflicted; he did not hide his face from me, but heard when I cried to him. From you comes my praise in the great congregation; my vows I will pay before those who fear him. The poor shall eat and be satisfied; those who seek him shall praise the Lord. May your hearts live forever!" – Psalm 22 (NRSV)

Reflection:
Psalm 22 is a deeply emotional psalm that begins with a cry of forsakenness and moves into expressions of trust and hope. David feels abandoned and overwhelmed by suffering, but he continues to appeal to God, trusting in His faithfulness and sovereignty. This psalm is often referred to as a Messianic psalm because it is closely linked with the suffering of Jesus on the cross. It speaks of deep distress but ultimately points to God's deliverance and faithfulness. The psalmist's journey from pain to praise reflects the hope that can emerge from even the darkest circumstances.

A Cry of Forsakenness
The psalm begins with a heart-wrenching cry, "My God, my God, why have you forsaken me?" David feels abandoned by God, and his emotional distress is palpable. This cry of abandonment is one that many believers have echoed in times of deep suffering. Yet, even in the midst of this raw despair, David still calls out to God, showing that even in the darkest moments, we can turn to God with our pain. Reflect on your own experiences of feeling distant from God. How can you bring your pain and frustration honestly before Him,

knowing that He hears you?

Related Verses:

- **Matthew 27:46** – "And about the ninth hour Jesus cried out with a loud voice, saying, 'My God, my God, why have you forsaken me?'"

- **Psalm 42:9-10** – "I say to God, my rock, 'Why have you forgotten me? Why must I go about mourning, oppressed by the enemy?'"

The Honesty of Suffering

David describes his suffering in vivid detail, expressing feelings of physical and emotional torment. He is mocked, rejected, and surrounded by enemies, and his body and soul are breaking down. His description of physical pain and spiritual abandonment foreshadows the suffering that Jesus would experience on the cross. In this psalm, we see that it is okay to express our raw emotions and to bring our suffering before God. Reflect on the times you have felt broken or forsaken. How can you allow your emotions to drive you toward God rather than away from Him?

Related Verses:

- **Romans 8:18** – "I consider that our present sufferings are not worth comparing with the glory that will be revealed in us."

- **Hebrews 4:15-16** – "For we do not have a high priest who is unable to sympathize with our weaknesses, but we have one who has been tempted in every way, just as we are—yet he did not sin. Let us then approach God's throne of grace with confidence, so that we may receive mercy and find grace to help us in our time of need."

The Hope of Deliverance

Amid the suffering, there is a turning point in the psalm. The psalmist begins to remind himself of God's past faithfulness, recalling how God has delivered His people in the past. He shifts from pleading to praising, declaring confidence that God will deliver him. This moment highlights the power of remembering God's past acts of faithfulness as a source of hope for the future. Reflect on times when God has been faithful to you. How can you use those memories to encourage your heart during difficult times?

Related Verses:

- **Psalm 34:6** – "This poor soul cried, and was heard by the Lord, and was saved from every trouble."

- **Isaiah 40:31** – "But those who hope in the Lord will renew their strength. They will soar on wings like eagles; they will run and not grow weary, they will walk and not be faint."

Praise and Thanksgiving

The psalm concludes with a declaration of praise. David commits to telling of God's name and praising Him before the congregation. Even in the midst of distress, David is confident that God will deliver him and that he will give thanks and praise for God's faithfulness. This turning to praise in the midst of suffering demonstrates the power of trusting God in our trials and declaring His goodness, even before we see the outcome. Reflect on how you can shift your focus from your circumstances to God's character, praising Him for who He is.

Related Verses:

- **Psalm 34:1** – "I will bless the Lord at all times; his praise shall continually be in my mouth."

- **Psalm 118:28-29** – "You are my God, and I will praise you; you are my God, and I will exalt you. Give thanks to the Lord, for he is good; his love endures forever."

Quote:
"God is not absent in our suffering. He is present with us in the midst of it, and His faithfulness is the anchor for our souls." – Max Lucado

---

Application:
In times of distress, it can feel as if God is far away, but Psalm 22 reminds us that God hears our cries, even when we feel forsaken. Like David, we can bring our pain and suffering before God, trusting that He is faithful to deliver and sustain us. Reflect on a current or past struggle where you can bring your pain to God, remembering His past faithfulness, and choose to praise Him, trusting that He will deliver.

Prayer:
Lord, I cry out to You in times of distress, knowing that You hear me even when I feel forsaken. Help me to bring my pain honestly before You and trust in Your faithfulness. Thank You for Your presence in the midst of suffering and for the hope of deliverance that You provide. I choose to praise You for who You are, my Redeemer and my Savior. Amen.

Memorization Guide:
Step 1: Break Down the Psalm into Sections
1. **Verses 1-2**: Cry of abandonment and distress.
2. **Verses 3-5**: Remembering God's faithfulness in the past.
3. **Verses 6-21**: Descriptions of suffering and plea for deliverance.

4. **Verses 22-31**: Turning to praise and thanksgiving for deliverance.

Step 2: Memorize by Key Themes and Visualizations

- **Section 1**: Crying out in distress (visualize calling out to God in deep pain).

- **Section 2**: Remembering God's faithfulness (visualize looking back on God's past deliverances).

- **Section 3**: Descriptions of suffering (visualize the heaviness of the psalmist's anguish).

- **Section 4**: Turning to praise (visualize lifting your hands in worship despite circumstances).

Verses:

- "My God, my God, why have you forsaken me?"

- "Yet you are holy, enthroned on the praises of Israel."

- "I will tell of your name to my brothers and sisters; in the midst of the congregation I will praise you."

- "The poor shall eat and be satisfied; those who seek him shall praise the Lord."

Step 3: Repetition and Recitation

1. Memorize one section at a time.

2. Gradually combine the sections into the full psalm.

3. Recite the psalm daily, visualizing the key themes.

Summary of Key Images:

- Crying out to God in distress.

- Remembering God's faithfulness.
- Describing suffering and pleading for deliverance.
- Turning to praise and thanksgiving.

Psalm 23 – The Lord is My Shepherd

"The Lord is my shepherd; I shall not want. He makes me lie down in green pastures. He leads me beside still waters; he restores my soul. He leads me in right paths for his name's sake. Even though I walk through the darkest valley, I fear no evil; for you are with me; your rod and your staff— they comfort me. You prepare a table before me in the presence of my enemies; you anoint my head with oil; my cup overflows. Surely goodness and mercy shall follow me all the days of my life, and I shall dwell in the house of the Lord my whole life long." – Psalm 23 (NRSV)

Reflection:

Psalm 23 is one of the most beloved and well-known psalms, providing comfort and assurance in God's care for His people. Through the metaphor of a shepherd, David describes God's attentive care, protection, and provision. In this psalm, we see a beautiful picture of God leading, guiding, and sustaining us through every season of life, including our darkest moments. It reminds us that we are never alone, for God's presence and provision will always sustain us. This psalm invites us to trust in God's goodness and faithfulness, knowing that He is always with us.

The Lord is My Shepherd

The psalm begins with a declaration of trust: "The Lord is my shepherd." David, a former shepherd, uses this intimate metaphor to describe God's relationship with His people. Just as a shepherd cares for his sheep, leading them to pasture and protecting them, so God leads us and cares for our needs. Reflect on what it means for God to be your

Shepherd. How does it comfort you to know that God is always with you, guiding you, and providing for you?

Related Verses:
- **John 10:11** – "I am the good shepherd. The good shepherd lays down his life for the sheep."
- **Isaiah 40:11** – "He will feed his flock like a shepherd; he will gather the lambs in his arms; he will carry them in his bosom, and gently lead those that are with young."

Provision and Rest

"He makes me lie down in green pastures. He leads me beside still waters; he restores my soul." These verses paint a picture of rest and peace. Just as sheep need peaceful pastures and still waters to be nourished and rested, so God provides for our needs—both physical and spiritual. He invites us to rest in Him, allowing Him to restore our soul. Reflect on how God has provided for your physical, emotional, or spiritual needs. In what areas of your life do you need to allow God to restore and refresh you?

Related Verses:
- **Matthew 11:28-30** – "Come to me, all you who are weary and burdened, and I will give you rest. Take my yoke upon you and learn from me, for I am gentle and humble in heart, and you will find rest for your souls."
- **Psalm 34:8** – "Oh, taste and see that the Lord is good! Blessed is the man who takes refuge in him."

Guidance and Righteous Paths

"He leads me in right paths for his name's sake." God does not only provide for us, but He also leads us on the right paths. His guidance is for His glory and for our good. God leads us into righteousness and His will for our lives. As we follow Him, He shapes us into the people He created us to be. Reflect on how God has guided you in your life. How can you more intentionally seek His guidance in your decisions and actions?

Related Verses:
- **Proverbs 3:5-6** – "Trust in the Lord with all your heart, and do not lean on your own understanding. In all your ways acknowledge him, and he will make straight your paths."
- **Isaiah 58:11** – "And the Lord will guide you continually and satisfy your desire in scorched places and make your bones strong; and you shall be like a watered garden, like a spring of water, whose waters do not fail."

Comfort in the Darkest Valley

"Even though I walk through the darkest valley, I fear no evil; for you are with me." This verse is one of the most comforting in all of Scripture. Even in the darkest and most difficult seasons of life, God is with us. He does not promise us that we will never face trouble, but He promises His presence and comfort through it all. Reflect on a time when you went through a dark season and experienced God's comforting presence. How does knowing that God is always with you impact your fear and anxiety in challenging times?

Related Verses:
- **Isaiah 43:2** – "When you pass through the waters, I will be with you; and through the rivers, they shall not overwhelm you; when you walk through fire you shall not be burned, and the flame shall not consume you."
- **2 Corinthians 1:3-4** – "Blessed be the God and Father of our Lord Jesus Christ, the Father of mercies and God of all comfort, who comforts us in all our affliction, so that we

may be able to comfort those who are in any affliction, with the comfort with which we ourselves are comforted by God."

God's Abundant Blessing

"You prepare a table before me in the presence of my enemies; you anoint my head with oil; my cup overflows." God's blessings are abundant. Even in the presence of enemies or difficulties, He prepares a feast for us, signifying His provision and care. The anointing of the head with oil symbolizes honor and blessing. Reflect on the blessings God has poured into your life, even in the midst of trials. How can you cultivate an attitude of gratitude for the abundance He has provided?

Related Verses:

- **Ephesians 1:3** – "Blessed be the God and Father of our Lord Jesus Christ, who has blessed us in Christ with every spiritual blessing in the heavenly places."

- **John 10:10** – "The thief comes only to steal and kill and destroy. I came that they may have life and have it abundantly."

Confidence in God's Goodness

"Surely goodness and mercy shall follow me all the days of my life, and I shall dwell in the house of the Lord my whole life long." The psalm ends with a confident declaration of God's goodness and faithfulness. David knows that God's mercy and goodness will always be with him, and he looks forward to dwelling in God's presence forever. Reflect on how you can cultivate a deeper trust in God's goodness. What does it mean for you to know that God's goodness and mercy follow you throughout your life?

Related Verses:
- **Psalm 34:6** – "This poor soul cried, and was heard by the Lord, and was saved from every trouble."
- **Revelation 21:3-4** – "And I heard a loud voice from the throne saying, 'See, the home of God is among mortals. He will dwell with them; they will be his peoples, and God himself will be with them; he will wipe every tear from their eyes. Death will be no more; mourning and crying and pain will be no more, for the first things have passed away.'"

Quote:
"The Lord is not my shepherd because of my goodness but because of His grace." – Charles Spurgeon

Application:
Psalm 23 is a reminder of God's constant care for His people. In moments of distress or confusion, we can rest in the knowledge that God is our Shepherd, leading us, comforting us, and providing for our needs. Take time today to reflect on how God has shepherded you in the past and how you can trust Him more fully in the future. Consider areas of your life where you need His guidance, comfort, or provision and bring those needs before Him in prayer.

Prayer:
Lord, You are my Shepherd, and I am grateful for Your care, provision, and guidance. Thank You for leading me beside still waters, for restoring my soul, and for being with me through every valley. I trust in Your goodness and mercy, knowing that they will follow me all the days of my life. Help

me to walk in Your ways and to find peace in Your presence. Amen.

Memorization Guide:

Step 1: Break Down the Psalm into Sections

1. **Verses 1-3**: The Lord as Shepherd providing care and rest.

2. **Verses 4-5**: Comfort in times of trouble and God's abundant blessing.

3. **Verse 6**: Confidence in God's goodness and the promise of eternal dwelling.

Step 2: Memorize by Key Themes and Visualizations

- **Section 1**: God as Shepherd (visualize being gently led by God to peaceful pastures).

- **Section 2**: Comfort and provision (visualize God preparing a feast for you in the midst of challenges).

- **Section 3**: Confidence in God's goodness (visualize walking with God, assured of His constant presence and care).

Verses:

- "The Lord is my shepherd; I shall not want."

- "Even though I walk through the darkest valley, I fear no evil; for you are with me."

- "Surely goodness and mercy shall follow me all the days of my life."

Step 3: Repetition and Recitation

1. Memorize one section at a time.

2. Gradually combine the sections into the full psalm.

3. Recite the psalm daily, visualizing the key themes.

Summary of Key Images:
- God as the Shepherd leading, providing, and protecting.
- Resting in God's peace and being restored.
- The abundance of God's blessings and His eternal presence.

Psalm 24 – The Lord's Sovereignty and Holiness

"The earth is the Lord's and the fullness thereof, the world and those who dwell therein; for he has founded it upon the seas and established it upon the rivers. Who shall ascend the hill of the Lord? And who shall stand in his holy place? He who has clean hands and a pure heart, who does not lift up his soul to what is false and does not swear deceitfully. He will receive blessing from the Lord and righteousness from the God of his salvation. Such is the generation of those who seek him, who seek the face of the God of Jacob. Selah. Lift up your heads, O gates! And be lifted up, O ancient doors, that the King of glory may come in. Who is this King of glory? The Lord, strong and mighty, the Lord, mighty in battle. Lift up your heads, O gates! And lift them up, O ancient doors, that the King of glory may come in. Who is this King of glory? The Lord of hosts, he is the King of glory! Selah." – Psalm 24 (NRSV)

Reflection:

Psalm 24 is a powerful psalm that begins with a declaration of God's sovereignty over all creation and ends with an invitation for the King of Glory to enter His people's lives. It beautifully highlights the Lord's rightful rule over the earth and emphasizes the holiness required to approach Him. This psalm calls us to examine our hearts and lives, to recognize God's supreme authority, and to seek His presence with purity and reverence.

The Earth Belongs to the Lord

The psalm opens with a statement of God's sovereignty: "The earth is the Lord's and the fullness thereof." Everything in creation belongs to God—He is the Creator, and all things exist for His glory. This reminds us that God is the ultimate authority over all things. Reflect on how you live in light of God's sovereignty. How do you honor God as the Creator and rightful ruler over the earth?

Related Verses:
- **Psalm 89:11** – "The heavens are yours, the earth also is yours; the world and all that is in it, you have founded them."
- **1 Corinthians 10:26** – "For 'the earth is the Lord's, and the fullness thereof.'"

Who Can Ascend the Hill of the Lord?

David then asks, "Who shall ascend the hill of the Lord?" This question invites us to consider who is worthy to enter God's holy presence. The answer is clear: those who have "clean hands and a pure heart." To approach God, we must be holy, free from sin, and devoted to truth. Reflect on the condition of your heart and actions. Are there areas where you need to repent and seek God's forgiveness, so you can approach Him with purity and integrity?

Related Verses:
- **Isaiah 33:14-15** – "Who among us can dwell with the consuming fire? Who among us can dwell with everlasting burnings? He who walks righteously and speaks uprightly, who despises the gain of oppression, who shakes his hands lest they hold a bribe, who stops his ears from hearing of bloodshed and shuts his eyes from looking on evil."
- **Matthew 5:8** – "Blessed are the pure in heart, for they shall see God."

The Blessing of Seeking God's Face

David goes on to explain that those who seek the Lord with clean hands and a pure heart will receive blessing and righteousness from the God of salvation. This highlights the beauty of seeking God—He blesses those who seek Him with sincerity. When we earnestly desire to be in God's presence and live according to His ways, He grants us righteousness and blessings. Reflect on how seeking God has brought blessings into your life. How can you prioritize seeking God's face with a pure heart?

Related Verses:
- **Jeremiah 29:13** – "You will seek me and find me, when you seek me with all your heart."
- **Matthew 7:7** – "Ask, and it will be given to you; seek, and you will find; knock, and it will be opened to you."

The King of Glory

The psalmist then shifts to a victorious declaration of the King of Glory. This section celebrates the majesty and strength of God as the King of Glory, who is mighty in battle. The imagery of gates and doors being lifted up symbolizes the anticipation of God's presence entering into our lives. It is a call for the people of God to prepare for His arrival, to make room for His glory in their hearts. Reflect on how you can prepare your heart to receive God's presence and honor Him as the King of Glory.

Related Verses:
- **Revelation 19:16** – "On his robe and on his thigh he has this name written: King of kings and Lord of lords."
- **Psalm 29:10** – "The Lord sits enthroned over the flood; the Lord sits enthroned as king forever."

The King of Hosts

The psalm concludes with a triumphant declaration: "The Lord of hosts, He is the King of glory!" The "Lord of hosts" refers to God's supreme power over all the heavenly armies, emphasizing His unmatched authority and majesty. God is not just the King of glory; He is the sovereign ruler over all creation, visible and invisible. Reflect on the vastness of God's reign. How does recognizing God as the Lord of hosts impact your understanding of His power and sovereignty?

Related Verses:

- **Isaiah 6:5** – "Woe is me! For I am lost; for I am a man of unclean lips, and I dwell in the midst of a people of unclean lips; for my eyes have seen the King, the Lord of hosts!"

- **Revelation 4:11** – "Worthy are you, our Lord and God, to receive glory and honor and power, for you created all things, and by your will they existed and were created."

Quote:
"God is not simply the King of our lives; He is the King of the universe, the Creator, and the ultimate ruler over everything. To honor Him as King is to acknowledge His supreme authority and our complete submission to His will." – Tony Evans

---

Application:
Psalm 24 calls us to recognize the greatness of God as the Creator and King of the universe. It challenges us to examine our hearts, ensuring that we approach God with purity and sincerity. Take time today to reflect on God's sovereignty. How can you better honor God as the King of Glory in your

daily life? Consider areas where you need to seek His presence more earnestly and prepare your heart to receive His glory.

Prayer:
Lord, You are the King of Glory, the Lord of hosts, and the Creator of all things. I acknowledge Your supreme authority over all creation and I submit myself to Your will. Cleanse my heart and help me to approach You with purity and sincerity. I seek Your presence, Lord, and I invite You to rule and reign in my life. May my life reflect Your majesty and glory. Amen.

Memorization Guide:
Step 1: Break Down the Psalm into Sections
1. **Verses 1-2**: God's sovereignty over the earth and creation.
2. **Verses 3-6**: The requirements for approaching God.
3. **Verses 7-10**: The celebration of the King of Glory.

Step 2: Memorize by Key Themes and Visualizations
- **Section 1**: God's sovereignty over creation (visualize God as Creator of all that is visible and invisible).
- **Section 2**: Purity required to approach God (visualize a pure heart and clean hands as you come into God's presence).
- **Section 3**: Celebrating the King of Glory (visualize the mighty King entering your heart and life with power and majesty).

Verses:

- "The earth is the Lord's and the fullness thereof, the world and those who dwell therein."

- "Who shall ascend the hill of the Lord? And who shall stand in his holy place?"

- "Lift up your heads, O gates! And be lifted up, O ancient doors, that the King of glory may come in."

- "The Lord of hosts, he is the King of glory!"

Step 3: Repetition and Recitation
1. Memorize one section at a time.
2. Gradually combine the sections into the full psalm.
3. Recite the psalm daily, visualizing the key themes.

Summary of Key Images:
- God's sovereignty over creation.
- The purity required to approach God's holy presence.
- The celebration of the King of Glory entering our lives.

Psalm 25 – A Prayer for Guidance and Forgiveness

"To you, O Lord, I lift up my soul. O my God, in you I trust; do not let me be put to shame; do not let my enemies exult over me. Do not let those who wait for you be put to shame; let them be ashamed who are wantonly treacherous. Make me to know your ways, O Lord; teach me your paths. Lead me in your truth, and teach me, for you are the God of my salvation; for you I wait all day long. Be mindful of your mercy, O Lord, and of your steadfast love, for they have been from of old. Do not remember the sins of my youth or my transgressions; according to your steadfast love remember me, for your goodness' sake, O Lord! Good and upright is the Lord; therefore he instructs sinners in the way. He leads the humble in what is right, and teaches the humble his way. All the paths of the Lord are steadfast love and faithfulness, for those who keep his covenant and his decrees. For your name's sake, O Lord, pardon my guilt, for it is great. Who are they that fear the Lord? He will teach them the way that they should choose. They will abide in prosperity, and their children shall possess the land. The friendship of the Lord is for those who fear him, and he makes his covenant known to them. My eyes are ever toward the Lord, for he will pluck my feet out of the net. Turn to me and be gracious to me, for I am lonely and afflicted. Relieve the troubles of my heart, and bring me out of my distress. Consider my affliction and my trouble, and forgive all my sins. Consider how many are my foes, and with what violent hatred they hate me. O guard my life, and deliver me; do not let me be put to shame, for I take refuge in you. May integrity and uprightness preserve me, for I wait for you. Redeem Israel, O God, out of all its troubles." – Psalm 25 (NRSV)

Reflection:

Psalm 25 is a heartfelt prayer of David, expressing his trust in God and his plea for guidance, forgiveness, and deliverance from his enemies. David's honest petition to God reflects the human longing for divine direction and help in times of difficulty. The psalm touches on themes of repentance, trust, and the hope that comes from knowing God's mercy and faithfulness. As we reflect on this psalm, we are reminded that God is faithful to guide us, forgive our sins, and lead us in the way of righteousness.

Trusting in God's Guidance

The psalm opens with a cry for God's guidance: "Make me to know your ways, O Lord; teach me your paths." David expresses a deep desire to follow God's direction, acknowledging that true wisdom comes from God alone. When faced with decisions or uncertainty, we can learn from David's example of seeking God's direction. Reflect on the areas of your life where you need God's guidance. Are there decisions or challenges where you can trust in God's leading and direction?

Related Verses:

- **Proverbs 3:5-6** – "Trust in the Lord with all your heart, and do not lean on your own understanding. In all your ways acknowledge him, and he will make straight your paths."

- **James 1:5** – "If any of you lacks wisdom, let him ask of God, who gives to all liberally and without reproach, and it will be given to him."

A Prayer for Forgiveness

David asks God not to remember the sins of his youth, but to remember him according to His steadfast love. This is a prayer of repentance and humility, acknowledging the need for God's forgiveness. Just as David recognized his need for God's mercy, we too must humble ourselves and seek forgiveness for the times we have fallen short. Reflect on any areas where you need God's forgiveness. How can you approach Him with a humble and repentant heart, trusting in His mercy?

Related Verses:

- **1 John 1:9** – "If we confess our sins, he is faithful and just to forgive us our sins and to cleanse us from all unrighteousness."

- **Psalm 51:10** – "Create in me a clean heart, O God, and renew a right spirit within me."

The Steadfast Love of the Lord

David reminds himself that all the paths of the Lord are filled with steadfast love and faithfulness. God's character is unchanging, and His ways are always rooted in love and truth. When we walk in God's ways, we can trust that He will lead us with faithfulness and compassion. Reflect on how you've experienced God's steadfast love in your life. How can you align your life more with His ways, knowing that His love is unshakeable?

Related Verses:

- **Psalm 36:5** – "Your steadfast love, O Lord, extends to the heavens, your faithfulness to the clouds."

- **Romans 8:39** – "Neither height nor depth, nor anything else in all creation, will be able to separate us from the love of God that is in Christ Jesus our Lord."

God as Our Protector

David's prayer is not only for guidance and forgiveness but also for protection. "My eyes are ever toward the Lord, for he will pluck my feet out of the net." David's confidence is in God's ability to protect him from harm and deliver him from his enemies. God is a refuge in times of trouble, and He will not leave us to face our difficulties alone. Reflect on how God has protected and delivered you. How can you continue to trust in His protection in the face of life's challenges?

Related Verses:

- **Psalm 91:4** – "He will cover you with his pinions, and under his wings you will find refuge; his faithfulness is a shield and buckler."

- **Isaiah 41:10** – "Fear not, for I am with you; be not dismayed, for I am your God; I will strengthen you, I will help you, I will uphold you with my righteous right hand."

The Hope of Redemption

Psalm 25 ends with a prayer for the redemption of Israel, acknowledging God's role as the ultimate deliverer. David's plea for redemption points to the broader hope of salvation that God offers to His people. Our ultimate redemption is found in Christ, who came to save us from sin and death. Reflect on the redemption God has already provided in your life. How can you live in response to the great salvation He has given us through Christ?

Related Verses:

- **Luke 1:68** – "Blessed be the Lord God of Israel, for he has visited and redeemed his people."

- **Romans 8:23** – "And not only the creation, but we ourselves, who have the firstfruits of the Spirit, groan inwardly as we wait eagerly for adoption as sons, the redemption of our bodies."

Quote:
"God's forgiveness is the great equalizer. No matter how far we have fallen, He is always ready to restore us to Himself." – Charles Stanley

Application:
Psalm 25 invites us to seek God's guidance, forgiveness, and protection while trusting in His steadfast love. Reflect on the areas of your life where you need God's direction, forgiveness, or deliverance. Bring those areas to Him in prayer, knowing that He is faithful to forgive and guide you. How can you actively seek God's wisdom and walk in His ways with humility, trusting that His mercy and goodness will follow you all the days of your life?

Prayer:
Lord, I lift up my soul to You. I trust in Your guidance, forgiveness, and protection. Please teach me Your ways, and help me to walk in righteousness. Cleanse me from my sins and lead me in Your truth. I trust in Your steadfast love and the hope of redemption You offer. Thank You for being my guide, my protector, and my Savior. Amen.

Memorization Guide:
Step 1: Break Down the Psalm into Sections
1. **Verses 1-7**: A plea for guidance and forgiveness.
2. **Verses 8-14**: God's goodness and faithfulness.

3. **Verses 15-22**: Prayer for protection and redemption.

Step 2: Memorize by Key Themes and Visualizations
- **Section 1**: Seeking God's guidance (visualize looking to God for wisdom).
- **Section 2**: Trusting in God's goodness and faithfulness (visualize God's unwavering love and truth).
- **Section 3**: Seeking God's protection and redemption (visualize God rescuing and redeeming you from difficulty).

Verses:
- "To you, O Lord, I lift up my soul."
- "Make me to know your ways, O Lord; teach me your paths."
- "All the paths of the Lord are steadfast love and faithfulness."
- "For your name's sake, O Lord, pardon my guilt, for it is great."

Step 3: Repetition and Recitation
1. Memorize one section at a time.
2. Gradually combine the sections into the full psalm.
3. Recite the psalm daily, visualizing the key themes.

Summary of Key Images:
- Seeking guidance and forgiveness from God.

- Trusting in God's goodness, faithfulness, and steadfast love.

- God as protector and redeemer in times of trouble.

Psalm 27 – Confidence in God's Protection

"The Lord is my light and my salvation; whom shall I fear? The Lord is the stronghold of my life; of whom shall I be afraid? When evildoers assail me to devour my flesh, my adversaries and foes, they shall stumble and fall. Though an army encamp against me, my heart shall not fear; though war arise against me, yet I will be confident. One thing I asked of the Lord, that will I seek after: to live in the house of the Lord all the days of my life, to behold the beauty of the Lord, and to inquire in his temple. For he will hide me in his shelter in the day of trouble; he will conceal me under the cover of his tent; he will set me high on a rock. Now my head is lifted up above my enemies all around me, and I will offer in his tent sacrifices with shouts of joy; I will sing and make melody to the Lord. Hear, O Lord, when I cry aloud, be gracious to me and answer me! 'Come,' my heart says, 'seek his face!' Your face, Lord, do I seek. Do not hide your face from me. Do not turn your servant away in anger, you who have been my help. Do not cast me off, do not forsake me, O God of my salvation! If my father and mother forsake me, the Lord will take me up. Teach me your way, O Lord, and lead me on a level path because of my enemies. Do not give me up to the will of my adversaries, for false witnesses have risen against me, and they are breathing out violence. I believe that I shall see the goodness of the Lord in the land of the living. Wait for the Lord; be strong, and let your heart take courage; wait for the Lord!" – Psalm 27 (NRSV)

Reflection:
Psalm 27 is a powerful psalm of trust, confidence, and longing for God's presence. David expresses his unwavering

confidence in God's protection and care, even in the face of overwhelming danger. Despite his enemies and the threats around him, David declares that the Lord is his light, salvation, and stronghold. This psalm not only reflects David's faith but also serves as an encouragement for us to trust in God's protection, seek His face, and wait on His timing. It's a reminder that in all circumstances, God is our refuge and the one who gives us strength.

The Lord is My Light and Salvation

The psalm begins with David's confident declaration that the Lord is his light and salvation. In a world filled with darkness, fear, and uncertainty, God is the light that dispels the darkness, and He is our salvation. David is not afraid because he trusts that God is the one who leads him and protects him. Reflect on what it means for God to be your light. In what areas of your life do you need God to shine His light, dispelling darkness and fear?

Related Verses:

- **John 8:12** – "Again Jesus spoke to them, saying, 'I am the light of the world. Whoever follows me will not walk in darkness, but will have the light of life.'"

- **Psalm 118:6** – "The Lord is on my side; I will not fear. What can man do to me?"

Confidence in the Face of Adversity

David expresses unwavering confidence in God, even when faced with an army of enemies. He declares, "Though an army encamp against me, my heart shall not fear." This speaks to David's trust in God's protection, knowing that even in the midst of danger, God is with him. Reflect on the times in your life when you have faced challenges or fears.

How can you build confidence in God's presence, knowing that He is always with you, no matter the situation?

Related Verses:
- **Isaiah 41:10** – "Fear not, for I am with you; be not dismayed, for I am your God; I will strengthen you, I will help you, I will uphold you with my righteous right hand."
- **Romans 8:31** – "What then shall we say to these things? If God is for us, who can be against us?"

Desire for God's Presence

David's desire in life is to dwell in God's house and behold His beauty. He longs to be in God's presence, to seek His face and inquire of Him. For David, the presence of God is more valuable than anything else. He desires intimacy with God above all else. Reflect on your own desire for God's presence. How often do you seek His face and spend time in His presence? How can you cultivate a deeper longing for God's fellowship in your life?

Related Verses:
- **Psalm 84:10** – "For a day in your courts is better than a thousand elsewhere. I would rather be a doorkeeper in the house of my God than dwell in the tents of wickedness."
- **Philippians 3:8** – "Indeed, I count everything as loss because of the surpassing worth of knowing Christ Jesus my Lord."

God as Our Refuge in Times of Trouble

David speaks of God's protection during times of trouble: "He will hide me in his shelter in the day of trouble." David trusts that in times of distress, God will provide a refuge, a safe place where he can find peace and security. This is an assurance for all who trust in God—that He will protect and sustain us in difficult times. Reflect on how God has been a refuge in your life. In times of fear, uncertainty, or trouble, how can you take refuge in God's presence?

Related Verses:

- **Psalm 46:1** – "God is our refuge and strength, a very present help in trouble."
- **Isaiah 25:4** – "For you have been a refuge to the poor, a refuge to the needy in their distress, a shelter from the storm and a shade from the heat."

A Prayer for Guidance

David asks God to teach him His ways and lead him on a level path. This request demonstrates David's dependence on God for guidance and direction. David's enemies seek to harm him, but he trusts that God will lead him away from danger and into righteousness. Reflect on how you can seek God's guidance in your own life. Are there areas where you need God's wisdom and direction?

Related Verses:

- **Proverbs 3:5-6** – "Trust in the Lord with all your heart, and do not lean on your own understanding. In all your ways acknowledge him, and he will make straight your paths."
- **Psalm 119:105** – "Your word is a lamp to my feet and a light to my path."

Hope and Confidence in God's Timing

David ends the psalm with a declaration of hope: "I believe that I shall see the goodness of the Lord in the land of the living." Even in the face of adversity, David holds onto the hope that God's goodness will prevail. This is a reminder that, no matter the situation, we can trust that God's goodness is always present and that He will bring about His perfect will in His perfect timing. Reflect on the hope you have in God's goodness. How does waiting on God build your trust in His timing and faithfulness?

Related Verses:
- **Romans 8:28** – "And we know that in all things God works for the good of those who love him, who have been called according to his purpose."
- **Lamentations 3:25** – "The Lord is good to those who wait for him, to the soul who seeks him."

Quote:
"In the midst of our struggles, we must remember that God is our refuge, and His goodness will prevail." – Charles Stanley

Application:
Psalm 27 is a powerful reminder that we can trust in God's protection, guidance, and presence, even in the most challenging circumstances. Reflect on how you can seek God's face more intentionally, trust Him in times of fear, and wait for His timing. Spend time today in prayer, asking God to guide you, protect you, and fill you with the confidence that comes from His presence.

Prayer:
Lord, You are my light, salvation, and stronghold. I trust in Your protection and Your ability to guide me through every trial. Teach me Your ways and lead me on a level path. Help me to seek Your presence above all else and to rest in the assurance of Your goodness and faithfulness. Thank You for

being my refuge and my help. I will wait for You, knowing that You are faithful to deliver. Amen.

Memorization Guide:

Step 1: Break Down the Psalm into Sections

1. **Verses 1-3**: Confidence in God's protection and salvation.

2. **Verses 4-6**: Desire for God's presence and guidance.

3. **Verses 7-14**: Prayer for help and confidence in God's timing.

Step 2: Memorize by Key Themes and Visualizations

- **Section 1**: God as our light and salvation (visualize God's light dispelling fear and darkness).

- **Section 2**: Seeking God's presence (visualize entering into the house of God, seeking His face).

- **Section 3**: Confidence in God's goodness (visualize waiting for God's perfect timing and trusting in His goodness).

Verses:

- "The Lord is my light and my salvation; whom shall I fear?"

- "One thing I asked of the Lord, that will I seek after: to live in the house of the Lord all the days of my life."

- "I believe that I shall see the goodness of the Lord in the land of the living."

- "Wait for the Lord; be strong, and let your heart take courage; wait for the Lord!"

Step 3: Repetition and Recitation

1. Memorize one section at a time.
2. Gradually combine the sections into the full psalm.
3. Recite the psalm daily, visualizing the key themes.

Summary of Key Images:
- God as our light, salvation, and refuge.
- Seeking God's presence with a pure heart.
- Confidence in God's protection, guidance, and timing.

Psalm 30 – Thanksgiving for God's Deliverance

"I will extol you, O Lord, for you have drawn me up and did not let my foes rejoice over me. O Lord my God, I cried to you for help, and you have healed me. O Lord, you brought up my soul from Sheol, restored me to life from among those gone down to the pit. Sing praises to the Lord, O you his faithful ones, and give thanks to his holy name. For his anger is but for a moment; his favor is for a lifetime. Weeping may linger for the night, but joy comes with the morning. As for me, I said in my prosperity, 'I shall never be moved.' By your favor, O Lord, you had established me as a strong mountain; you hid your face; I was dismayed. To you, O Lord, I cried, and to the Lord I made supplication: 'What profit is there in my death, if I go down to the pit? Will the dust praise you? Will it tell of your faithfulness? Hear, O Lord, and be gracious to me! O Lord, be my helper!' You have turned my mourning into dancing; you have taken off my sackcloth and clothed me with joy, so that my soul may praise you and not be silent. O Lord my God, I will give thanks to you forever." – Psalm 30 (NRSV)

Reflection:
Psalm 30 is a psalm of thanksgiving, a song of praise to God for His deliverance and mercy. David begins by recounting the great deliverance God has brought him, lifting him from the depths of despair and restoring his life. The psalm reflects a journey from weeping to joy, from mourning to dancing. It is a celebration of God's faithfulness and a reminder of the power of God to transform even the darkest moments into times of rejoicing. This psalm calls us to reflect on God's faithfulness in our lives and to respond with thanksgiving and praise.

A Cry for Help and God's Healing
David begins by acknowledging that he cried out to God for help and that God answered by healing him. The psalmist's plea for help is met with God's compassion and healing power. Reflect on the times when you've cried out to God in desperation, and consider how He has answered you. How has God healed you—whether physically, emotionally, or spiritually?

Related Verses:
- **Psalm 34:6** – "This poor soul cried, and was heard by the Lord, and was saved from every trouble."
- **Jeremiah 30:17** – "For I will restore health to you, and your wounds I will heal, declares the Lord."

Weeping and Rejoicing
David contrasts the weeping that may last through the night with the joy that comes in the morning. This powerful metaphor highlights the temporary nature of sorrow and the certainty of God's joy after suffering. While we may endure seasons of mourning, God promises to bring joy and

restoration. Reflect on how you've experienced seasons of weeping, but also how God has brought you joy and peace after hardship. How can you trust in God's promise of joy in the morning?

Related Verses:

- **2 Corinthians 4:17** – "For this light momentary affliction is preparing for us an eternal weight of glory beyond all comparison."

- **Romans 8:18** – "For I consider that the sufferings of this present time are not worth comparing with the glory that is to be revealed to us."

The Danger of Pride and the Need for God's Help

David reflects on a time when he felt secure in his prosperity, saying, "I shall never be moved." But when God hid His face, David was dismayed. This moment serves as a reminder of the dangers of pride and self-sufficiency. When things are going well, it's easy to forget our dependence on God, but David shows us the importance of crying out to God, especially in moments of hardship. Reflect on your own moments of self-reliance. How can you cultivate a heart of humility, always recognizing your need for God's help and favor?

Related Vers

- **Proverbs 16:18** – "Pride goes before destruction, and a haughty spirit before a fall."

- **Psalm 131:1** – "O Lord, my heart is not lifted up; my eyes are not raised too high; I do not occupy myself with things too great and too marvelous for me."

God Turns Mourning into Dancing

One of the most beautiful verses in this psalm is when David acknowledges how God has transformed his mourning into dancing. God has replaced his sackcloth, a symbol of mourning, with joy. This is a picture of the transformative power of God, who not only heals but also brings joy and celebration where there was once sorrow. Reflect on how God has turned your mourning into dancing, even if it was gradual. How can you actively praise God for the ways He has restored joy in your life?

Related Verses:
- **Isaiah 61:3** – "To grant to those who mourn in Zion—to give them a beautiful headdress instead of ashes, the oil of gladness instead of mourning, the garment of praise instead of a faint spirit."
- **Zephaniah 3:17** – "The Lord your God is in your midst, a mighty one who will save; he will rejoice over you with gladness; he will quiet you by his love; he will exult over you with loud singing."

Thanksgiving and Praise

The psalm concludes with David committing to give thanks to God forever. David's response to God's deliverance is a life of gratitude, praise, and worship. This is a reminder that when we experience God's goodness, it should move us to praise Him continually. Reflect on the ways you can express your gratitude to God today. How can you cultivate a life of ongoing thanksgiving, not just in moments of deliverance but in all circumstances?

Related Verses:
- **Psalm 106:1** – "Praise the Lord! Oh give thanks to the Lord, for he is good, for his steadfast love endures forever."

- **1 Thessalonians 5:18** – "Give thanks in all circumstances; for this is the will of God in Christ Jesus for you."

Quote:
"In times of despair, we can be confident that God will not leave us in our sorrow but will bring joy in the morning, transforming our mourning into dancing." – Charles Spurgeon

Application:
Psalm 30 is a beautiful reminder of the transforming power of God. It calls us to reflect on times when we have experienced sorrow, but also how God has been faithful to bring joy and restoration. Spend some time today thanking God for the ways He has delivered and restored you. Even if you are going through a difficult season, trust that God will bring joy in His time. How can you express your gratitude to God for His healing, provision, and love?

Prayer:
Lord, I will extol You for You have drawn me up and delivered me from the depths. Thank You for turning my mourning into dancing and for replacing my sorrow with joy. Help me to continually seek Your presence and give You thanks, even in times of difficulty. I trust in Your faithfulness and Your ability to transform every circumstance for Your glory. May my life be a constant song of praise to You. Amen.

Memorization Guide:
Step 1: Break Down the Psalm into Sections
1. **Verses 1-3**: Thanksgiving for deliverance and healing.
2. **Verses 4-5**: Trust in God's timing for joy after sorrow.

3. **Verses 6-10**: Reflection on God's help and David's prayer for mercy.
4. **Verses 11-12**: Celebration of God's transformation and a life of praise.

Step 2: Memorize by Key Themes and Visualizations

- **Section 1**: Thanksgiving for deliverance (visualize crying out to God and experiencing His healing).
- **Section 2**: Trusting in God's timing (visualize waiting for joy after the night of weeping).
- **Section 3**: Seeking God's mercy (visualize asking God for help and mercy during difficult times).
- **Section 4**: Celebrating transformation (visualize dancing in joy as God turns mourning into celebration).

Verses:

- "I will extol you, O Lord, for you have drawn me up."
- "Weeping may linger for the night, but joy comes with the morning."
- "You have turned my mourning into dancing; you have taken off my sackcloth and clothed me with joy."

Step 3: Repetition and Recitation

1. Memorize one section at a time.
2. Gradually combine the sections into the full psalm.
3. Recite the psalm daily, visualizing the key themes.

Summary of Key Images:

- Crying out to God for deliverance and experiencing His healing.

- Trusting in God's timing for joy after sorrow.

- Dancing in joy after mourning.

- Living a life of continual praise and gratitude.

Psalm 31 – A Prayer for Deliverance and Trust in God

"In you, O Lord, I seek refuge; do not let me ever be put to shame; in your righteousness deliver me. Incline your ear to me; rescue me speedily. Be a rock of refuge for me, a strong fortress to save me. You are indeed my rock and my fortress; for your name's sake lead me and guide me, take me out of the net that is hidden for me, for you are my refuge. Into your hand I commit my spirit; you have redeemed me, O Lord, faithful God. You hate those who pay regard to worthless idols, but I trust in the Lord. I will exult and rejoice in your steadfast love, because you have seen my affliction; you have taken heed of my adversities, and have not delivered me into the hand of the enemy; you have set my feet in a broad place. Be gracious to me, O Lord, for I am in distress; my eye wastes away from grief, my soul and body also. For my life is spent with sorrow, and my years with sighing; my strength fails because of my misery, and my bones waste away. I am the scorn of all my adversaries, a horror to my neighbors, an object of dread to my acquaintances; those who see me in the street flee from me. I have passed out of mind like one who is dead; I have become like a broken vessel. For I hear the whispering of many—terror all around—as they scheme together against me, as they plot to take my life. But I trust in you, O Lord; I say, 'You are my God.' My times are in your hand; deliver me from the hand of my enemies and persecutors. Let your face shine upon your servant; save me in your steadfast love. Do not let me be put to shame, O Lord, for I call on you; let the wicked be put to shame; let them go silently to Sheol. Let the lying lips be dumb, which speak insolently against the righteous with pride and contempt. O how abundant is your goodness, which you have laid up for those who fear you, and accomplished for those who take refuge in you, in the sight of everyone! In the shelter of your presence you hide them from human plots; you hold them safe under your shelter from contentious tongues. Blessed be the Lord, for he has wondrously shown his steadfast love to me when I was beset as a city under siege. I had said in my alarm, 'I am driven far from your sight.' But you heard my supplications when I cried to you for help. Love the Lord, all you his saints. The Lord preserves the faithful, but abundantly repays the one who acts haughtily. Be strong, and let your heart take courage, all you who wait for the Lord!" – Psalm 31 (NRSV)

Reflection:
Psalm 31 is a heartfelt prayer of David, who cries out to God for refuge, deliverance, and help during times of distress and deep sorrow. In this psalm, David faces enemies and overwhelming adversity, but he continually places his trust in God, knowing that His steadfast love and faithfulness will guide and protect him. Despite the overwhelming challenges, David's prayer is filled with trust in God's timing and mercy. This psalm is a powerful reminder that, in times of trial, we can always seek refuge in God, trusting that He will deliver and protect us.

Seeking Refuge in God
David begins by calling out to God as his refuge, asking to be delivered from his enemies and trials. He recognizes God as his rock and fortress, the one who protects him from harm. In the midst of challenges, David finds peace in God's protection, and we are reminded to do the same when we face difficulty. Reflect on areas of your life where you need

God to be your refuge. How can you more fully trust God to protect you during times of distress?

Related Verses:

- **Psalm 91:2** – "I will say to the Lord, 'My refuge and my fortress, my God, in whom I trust.'"
- **Proverbs 18:10** – "The name of the Lord is a strong tower; the righteous run into it and are safe."

Trusting God in Times of Distress

David acknowledges his deep sorrow and affliction, but he continues to trust in God's love and faithfulness. He expresses his emotional and physical exhaustion but still maintains hope in God's care. Even when we experience suffering, it's important to trust that God sees our affliction and will not abandon us. Reflect on how God has been faithful to you in difficult times. How can you continue to trust Him, even when circumstances seem overwhelming?

Related Verses:

- **Isaiah 41:10** – "Fear not, for I am with you; be not dismayed, for I am your God; I will strengthen you, I will help you, I will uphold you with my righteous right hand."
- **2 Corinthians 1:3-4** – "Blessed be the God and Father of our Lord Jesus Christ, the Father of mercies and God of all comfort, who comforts us in all our affliction, so that we may be able to comfort those who are in any affliction, with the comfort with which we ourselves are comforted by God."

God's Steadfast Love and Protection

David rejoices in God's steadfast love, acknowledging that God has shown His kindness and mercy even in times of hardship. He praises God for His protection and deliverance, especially when facing adversity. The psalm reflects how God's goodness is abundant for those who fear Him, and He is our shelter and safety. Reflect on how you have experienced God's steadfast love. How can you express gratitude for His faithfulness and seek refuge in His presence?

Related Verses:
- **Romans 8:39** – "Neither height nor depth, nor anything else in all creation, will be able to separate us from the love of God that is in Christ Jesus our Lord."
- **Psalm 36:7** – "How precious is your steadfast love, O God! The children of mankind take refuge in the shadow of your wings."

The Power of Trusting God's Timing

David expresses his trust in God's timing, declaring that his times are in God's hands. Even when it feels like everything is out of control, David recognizes that God is sovereign over all things, and His timing is perfect. Reflect on how trusting God's timing has helped you in your life. Are there areas where you need to surrender control and trust that God will act in His perfect time?

Related Verses:
- **Ecclesiastes 3:1** – "For everything there is a season, and a time for every matter under heaven."
- **Psalm 31:15** – "My times are in your hand; rescue me from the hand of my enemies and from my persecutors."

Encouragement to Wait on the Lord

The psalm concludes with an encouragement to be strong and take courage while waiting on the Lord. David calls on all the faithful to love the Lord and wait for His deliverance. When we wait on God, we are assured that He will preserve us, and He will answer in His time. Reflect on the areas of your life where you need courage to wait for God's response. How can you strengthen your heart as you wait for His deliverance?

Related Verses:

- **Isaiah 40:31** – "But they who wait for the Lord shall renew their strength; they shall mount up with wings like eagles; they shall run and not be weary; they shall walk and not faint."

- **Lamentations 3:25-26** – "The Lord is good to those who wait for him, to the soul who seeks him. It is good that one should wait quietly for the salvation of the Lord."

Quote:
"Trusting in God during times of distress doesn't mean we won't feel the pain, but it means we trust He will deliver us in His perfect time." – Billy Graham

Application:
Psalm 31 teaches us how to trust God in times of distress, seek refuge in His presence, and wait for His deliverance. Take time today to reflect on areas where you are experiencing difficulty or uncertainty. Bring these areas to God, acknowledging your trust in His timing and sovereignty. Seek His refuge and comfort, knowing that He is always faithful to protect, deliver, and show His steadfast love.

Prayer:
Lord, You are my refuge and my fortress. I trust in Your timing and Your goodness, even when I face adversity. Help me to

seek Your presence and find comfort in Your steadfast love. Teach me to wait for You with courage, knowing that You will deliver me in Your perfect time. Thank You for being my protector, my healer, and my Savior. Amen.

Memorization Guide:

Step 1: Break Down the Psalm into Sections

1. **Verses 1-8**: Cry for help and confidence in God's protection.

2. **Verses 9-18**: Plea for mercy, trust in God's timing.

3. **Verses 19-24**: Praise for God's deliverance and encouragement to trust.

Step 2: Memorize by Key Themes and Visualizations

- **Section 1**: Seeking refuge in God (visualize running to God as your safe place).

- **Section 2**: Trusting God's mercy and timing (visualize waiting for God's perfect timing).

- **Section 3**: Rejoicing in God's deliverance (visualize celebrating God's faithfulness).

Verses:

- "In you, O Lord, I seek refuge; do not let me ever be put to shame."

- "I will exult and rejoice in your steadfast love, because you have seen my affliction."

- "Be strong, and let your heart take courage, all you who wait for the Lord!"

Step 3: Repetition and Recitation

1. Memorize one section at a time.
2. Gradually combine the sections into the full psalm.
3. Recite the psalm daily, visualizing the key themes.

Summary of Key Images:

- Seeking God as our refuge and protector.
- Trusting in God's timing for deliverance.
- Rejoicing in God's steadfast love and faithfulness.

Psalm 33 – Praise for God's Faithfulness and Power

"Rejoice in the Lord, O you righteous. Praise befits the upright. Give thanks to the Lord with the lyre; make melody to him with the harp of ten strings. Sing to him a new song; play skillfully on the strings, with loud shouts. For the word of the Lord is upright, and all his work is done in faithfulness. He loves righteousness and justice; the earth is full of the steadfast love of the Lord. By the word of the Lord the heavens were made, and all their host by the breath of his mouth. He gathered the waters of the sea as in a bottle; he put the deeps in storehouses. Let all the earth fear the Lord; let all the inhabitants of the world stand in awe of him. For he spoke, and it came to be; he commanded, and it stood firm. The Lord brings the counsel of the nations to nothing; he frustrates the plans of the peoples. The counsel of the Lord stands forever, the thoughts of his heart to all generations. Happy is the nation whose God is the Lord, the people whom he has chosen as his heritage. The Lord looks down from heaven; he sees all humankind. From where he sits enthroned he watches all the inhabitants of the earth— he who fashions the hearts of them all and observes all their deeds. A king is not saved by his great army; a warrior is not delivered by his great strength. The war horse is a vain hope for victory, and by its great might it cannot save. Truly the eye of the Lord is on those who fear him, on those who hope in his steadfast love, to deliver their soul from death, and to keep them alive in famine. Our soul waits for the Lord; he is our help and our shield. Our heart is glad in him, because we trust in his holy name. Let your steadfast love, O Lord, be upon us, even as we hope in you." – Psalm 33 (NRSV)

Reflection:
Psalm 33 is a psalm of praise that celebrates God's power as

Creator and His sovereignty over all things. The psalmist invites all the righteous to rejoice in the Lord, recognizing His faithfulness, righteousness, and love. In a world filled with uncertainty and shifting powers, this psalm reminds us that God's Word is trustworthy, and His plans stand firm. God is the Creator of the universe, and His wisdom and counsel are unchanging. This psalm calls us to recognize God's authority, trust in His protection, and celebrate His steadfast love, which is shown to all who hope in Him.

Rejoicing in God's Faithfulness

David begins by calling on the righteous to rejoice in the Lord, for God's praise is befitting to the upright. Rejoicing in God is a natural response to His faithfulness and righteousness. Praise is not just for the great moments in life, but it is a continual act of recognizing God's goodness in all circumstances. Reflect on how you can cultivate a lifestyle of praise, whether in good times or bad. How can you practice gratitude and praise for God's righteousness and faithfulness?

Related Verses:

- **Psalm 92:1-2** – "It is good to give thanks to the Lord, to sing praises to your name, O Most High, to declare your steadfast love in the morning, and your faithfulness by night."

- **Philippians 4:4** – "Rejoice in the Lord always; again I will say, Rejoice."

The Word of the Lord Is Upright

The psalmist declares that the word of the Lord is upright, and all His work is done in faithfulness. God's Word is true and trustworthy. When we place our hope in His promises, we can be confident that He will fulfill them. Reflect on the promises of God found in Scripture. How has God's Word proven true in your life? How can you anchor your faith in His reliable promises?

Related Verses:
- **Isaiah 55:11** – "So shall my word be that goes out from my mouth; it shall not return to me empty, but it shall accomplish that which I purpose, and shall succeed in the thing for which I sent it."
- **2 Corinthians 1:20** – "For all the promises of God find their Yes in him. That is why it is through him that we utter our Amen to God for his glory."

God as the Creator of All

The psalmist gives a magnificent description of God's power as Creator. He speaks, and creation comes into being. The vastness of the heavens and the power of the seas are under His command. God is not just a distant Creator; He is intimately involved with His creation. Reflect on the greatness of God as Creator. How does the natural world speak to you of God's power and majesty? Take time today to appreciate the beauty of creation as a reflection of God's glory.

Related Verses:
- **Genesis 1:1** – "In the beginning, God created the heavens and the earth."
- **Romans 1:20** – "For his invisible attributes, namely, his eternal power and divine nature, have been clearly perceived, ever since the creation of the world, in the things that have been made."

The Sovereignty of God Over Nations

God's sovereignty is a recurring theme in this psalm. The psalmist proclaims that while the plans of nations and rulers may fail,

God's counsel stands forever. His purposes will always prevail. This is a comforting reminder that, no matter how chaotic or uncertain the world may seem, God remains in control. Reflect on the global challenges and uncertainties you may face. How can you rest in the assurance that God's plans are unshakable and eternal?

Related Verses:

- **Isaiah 46:10** – "Declaring the end from the beginning and from ancient times things not yet done, saying, 'My counsel shall stand, and I will accomplish all my purpose.'"

- **Proverbs 19:21** – "Many are the plans in the mind of a man, but it is the purpose of the Lord that will stand."

Trusting in God's Protection

The psalmist emphasizes that the Lord's eye is on those who fear Him and hope in His steadfast love. God protects His people, delivering them from death and sustaining them through famine. In a world filled with dangers and challenges, it is a great comfort to know that God watches over us and provides for us. Reflect on the ways God has protected and provided for you. How can you grow in trusting God's protection and care for you, even in difficult circumstances?

Related Verses:

- **Psalm 121:3-4** – "He will not let your foot be moved; he who keeps you will not slumber. Behold, he who keeps Israel will neither slumber nor sleep."

- **Matthew 6:26** – "Look at the birds of the air: they neither sow nor reap nor gather into barns, and yet your heavenly Father feeds them. Are you not of more value than they?"

Waiting on the Lord

The psalm ends with an encouragement to wait for the Lord, to be strong and take courage. Waiting on God requires patience and trust in His timing, knowing that He is working behind the scenes for our good. Reflect on the areas of your life where you need to wait for God's guidance or timing. How can you find strength and courage while you wait, trusting that God will act in His perfect time?

Related Verses:
- **Isaiah 40:31** – "But they who wait for the Lord shall renew their strength; they shall mount up with wings like eagles; they shall run and not be weary; they shall walk and not faint."
- **Psalm 27:14** – "Wait for the Lord; be strong, and let your heart take courage; wait for the Lord!"

Quote:

"When we wait on God, we are not passive; we are actively trusting, hoping, and relying on His timing and purposes." – John Piper

Application:

Psalm 33 calls us to rejoice in God's faithfulness and power, acknowledging His sovereignty over all things and trusting in His protection and provision. Take time today to reflect on the areas where you can rejoice in God's work, trust in His Word, and wait for His perfect timing. Praise God for His sovereignty and commit to trusting Him in every area of your life, knowing that He will act for your good and His glory.

Prayer:

After HIS Own Heart

Lord, I praise You for Your greatness as the Creator of the heavens and the earth. I trust in Your sovereignty, knowing that Your plans will always prevail. Help me to rest in Your faithfulness and to wait for You with patience and trust. Thank You for Your protection and provision in my life. May my heart always rejoice in Your goodness and Your love. Amen.

Memorization Guide:

Step 1: Break Down the Psalm into Sections

1. **Verses 1-3**: A call to praise and thanksgiving.
2. **Verses 4-9**: God's power as Creator and Sovereign.
3. **Verses 10-17**: The futility of human strength and the Lord's protection.
4. **Verses 18-22**: Trusting in God's protection and waiting for Him.

Step 2: Memorize by Key Themes and Visualizations

- **Section 1**: Rejoicing in God's faithfulness (visualize lifting up your hands in praise).
- **Section 2**: Recognizing God's sovereignty (visualize God speaking creation into existence).
- **Section 3**: Trusting in God's protection (visualize God's watchful eye over you).
- **Section 4**: Waiting for God's timing (visualize patiently trusting in God's plan).

Verses:

- "Rejoice in the Lord, O you righteous. Praise befits the upright."

- "The word of the Lord is upright, and all his work is done in faithfulness."
- "Our heart is glad in him, because we trust in his holy name."
- "Let your steadfast love, O Lord, be upon us, even as we hope in you."

Step 3: Repetition and Recitation
1. Memorize one section at a time.
2. Gradually combine the sections into the full psalm.
3. Recite the psalm daily, visualizing the key themes.

Summary of Key Images:
- Praising God for His greatness and faithfulness.
- Recognizing God's sovereignty over creation and nations.
- Trusting in God's protection and provision.
- Waiting for God's timing and deliverance.

Psalm 34 – A Call to Praise and Trust in God's Deliverance

"I will bless the Lord at all times; his praise shall continually be in my mouth. My soul makes its boast in the Lord; let the humble hear and be glad. O magnify the Lord with me, and let us exalt his name together. I sought the Lord, and he answered me, and delivered me from all my fears. Look to him, and be radiant; so your faces shall never be ashamed. This poor soul cried, and was heard by the Lord, and was saved from every trouble. The angel of the Lord encamps around those who fear him, and delivers them. O taste and see that the Lord is good; happy are those who take refuge in him. O fear the Lord, you his holy ones, for those who fear him have no want. The young lions suffer want and hunger, but those who seek the Lord lack no good thing. Come, O children, listen to me; I will teach you the fear of the Lord. Which of you desires life, and covets many days to enjoy good? Keep your tongue from evil, and your lips from speaking deceit. Depart from evil, and do good; seek peace, and pursue it. The eyes of the Lord are on the righteous, and his ears are open to their cry. The face of the Lord is against evildoers, to cut off the memory of them from the earth. When the righteous cry for help, the Lord hears, and rescues them from all their troubles. The Lord is near to the brokenhearted, and saves the crushed in spirit. Many are the afflictions of the righteous, but the Lord rescues them from them all. He keeps all their bones; not one of them will be broken. Evil brings death to the wicked, and those who hate the righteous will be condemned. The Lord redeems the life of his servants; none of those who take refuge in him will be condemned." – Psalm 34 (NRSV)

Reflection:

Psalm 34 is a psalm of thanksgiving and praise, where David expresses his gratitude to God for His deliverance and faithfulness. This psalm highlights the importance of seeking God, trusting in His goodness, and living in alignment with His will. David's personal testimony of God's faithfulness invites us to rejoice in God's constant presence and protection. The psalm encourages us to seek peace, trust in God's goodness, and remember that God is near to those who are brokenhearted. It's a call to praise God for His deliverance and to live a life of integrity and trust.

Blessing the Lord at All Times
David begins by stating that he will bless the Lord "at all times," and his praise will continually be on his lips. This declaration reflects an attitude of constant gratitude and worship, not dependent on circumstances but rooted in the nature of God. Reflect on your own approach to worship and praise. Do you praise God in all circumstances, or are there moments when you forget His goodness? How can you cultivate a lifestyle of praise, regardless of your current situation?

Related Verses:
- **1 Thessalonians 5:16-18** – "Rejoice always, pray without ceasing, give thanks in all circumstances; for this is the will of God in Christ Jesus for you."

- **Psalm 71:6** – "Upon you I have leaned from my birth; it was you who took me from my mother's womb. My praise is continually of you."

Seeking the Lord's Deliverance
David testifies that when he sought the Lord, God answered him and delivered him from all his fears. God's faithfulness is evident in His responsiveness to our cries for help. Reflect on times in your life when you sought God's help, and He answered. How did

God deliver you from fear or anxiety? How can you continue to seek God in times of trouble, knowing that He hears and responds to the prayers of His people?

Related Verses:

- **Jeremiah 33:3** – "Call to me and I will answer you, and will tell you great and hidden things that you have not known."
- **Philippians 4:6-7** – "Do not be anxious about anything, but in everything by prayer and supplication with thanksgiving let your requests be made known to God. And the peace of God, which surpasses all understanding, will guard your hearts and your minds in Christ Jesus."

Taste and See that the Lord is Good

David invites us to "taste and see that the Lord is good." This is an invitation to experience God's goodness firsthand. Just as we taste food to experience its flavor, we are invited to experience God's goodness through His faithfulness in our lives. Reflect on how you have experienced God's goodness. How has God shown Himself to be faithful, loving, and good in your life? Consider how you can share that goodness with others as a testimony of His faithfulness.

Related Verses:

- **Psalm 36:8** – "They feast on the abundance of your house, and you give them drink from the river of your delights."
- **Romans 8:32** – "He who did not spare his own Son but gave him up for us all, how will he not also with him graciously give us all things?"

Living in the Fear of the Lord

David instructs us to live in the fear of the Lord, which includes avoiding evil, speaking truth, and seeking peace. The "fear of the Lord" is not a terror but a reverence and awe that leads to a life of righteousness. Reflect on what it means to live in the fear of the Lord. How can you pursue peace, speak truth, and avoid evil in your relationships and actions?

Related Verses:
- **Proverbs 9:10** – "The fear of the Lord is the beginning of wisdom, and the knowledge of the Holy One is insight."
- **Matthew 5:9** – "Blessed are the peacemakers, for they shall be called sons of God."

God's Nearness to the Brokenhearted

One of the most beautiful promises in Psalm 34 is that "the Lord is near to the brokenhearted and saves the crushed in spirit." God's nearness to us in our times of emotional and spiritual distress is a powerful reminder of His love and care. Reflect on how God has been near to you in your moments of brokenness. How can you open your heart to His healing and comforting presence when you feel brokenhearted?

Related Verses:
- **Psalm 147:3** – "He heals the brokenhearted and binds up their wounds."
- **Isaiah 57:15** – "For thus says the One who is high and lifted up, who inhabits eternity, whose name is Holy: 'I dwell in the high and holy place, and also with him who is of a contrite and lowly spirit, to revive the spirit of the lowly, and to revive the heart of the contrite.'"

The Lord's Protection and Deliverance

David concludes by praising God for His protection and deliverance. He acknowledges that God's protection is not only for the righteous but also for those who take refuge in Him. This is a reminder that God rescues us from the dangers of the world, and He preserves our lives. Reflect on how God has protected you in times of danger or hardship. How can you trust Him more fully as your protector in every season of life?

Related Verses:
- **Psalm 91:14-15** – "Because he holds fast to me in love, I will deliver him; I will protect him, because he knows my name. When he calls to me, I will answer him; I will be with him in trouble; I will rescue him and honor him."
- **Romans 8:31** – "What then shall we say to these things? If God is for us, who can be against us?"

Quote:
"When we seek God's presence, He meets us with His goodness. His goodness is more than enough to heal our hearts and transform our lives." – Anne Graham Lotz

Application:
Psalm 34 invites us to rejoice in God's goodness, trust in His protection, and seek His presence. Take time today to reflect on God's faithfulness in your life. Praise Him for His goodness and seek His presence in your daily walk. As you face challenges, trust in God's promise to be near to the brokenhearted and to rescue you from trouble. How can you live in the fear of the Lord, speak truth, and pursue peace today?

Prayer:
Lord, I praise You for Your goodness, faithfulness, and deliverance. Thank You for being near to me in times of trouble and for rescuing me when I call out to You. Help me to live in reverence and awe of You, seeking Your presence and trusting

in Your protection. May my life reflect Your goodness and love to those around me. Amen.

Memorization Guide:

Step 1: Break Down the Psalm into Sections

1. **Verses 1-3**: A call to praise and thanksgiving.
2. **Verses 4-7**: Trusting in God's deliverance.
3. **Verses 8-14**: Living in the fear of the Lord.
4. **Verses 15-22**: God's nearness, protection, and deliverance.

Step 2: Memorize by Key Themes and Visualizations

- **Section 1**: Praising God for His goodness (visualize lifting your hands in praise to God).
- **Section 2**: Trusting in God's deliverance (visualize crying out to God and experiencing His rescue).
- **Section 3**: Living in reverence of the Lord (visualize choosing peace, truth, and righteousness).
- **Section 4**: Finding refuge in God's protection (visualize taking shelter under God's wings).

Verses:

- "I will bless the Lord at all times; his praise shall continually be in my mouth."
- "O taste and see that the Lord is good; happy are those who take refuge in him."
- "The eyes of the Lord are on the righteous, and his ears are open to their cry."

- "The Lord redeems the life of his servants; none of those who take refuge in him will be condemned."

Step 3: Repetition and Recitation
1. Memorize one section at a time.
2. Gradually combine the sections into the full psalm.
3. Recite the psalm daily, visualizing the key themes.

Summary of Key Images:
- Rejoicing and praising God for His goodness.
- Seeking God's refuge and trusting in His deliverance.
- Living in reverence of the Lord and pursuing righteousness.
- Finding shelter under God's protection and love.

Psalm 37 – Trusting God in the Face of Injustice

"Do not fret because of the wicked; do not be envious of wrongdoers, for they will soon fade like the grass, and wither like the green herb. Trust in the Lord, and do good; so you will live in the land, and enjoy security. Take delight in the Lord, and he will give you the desires of your heart. Commit your way to the Lord; trust in him, and he will act. He will make your vindication shine like the light, and the justice of your cause like the noonday. Be still before the Lord, and wait patiently for him; do not fret over those who prosper in their way, over those who carry out evil devices. Refrain from anger, and forsake wrath. Do not fret—it leads only to evil. For the wicked shall be cut off, but those who wait for the Lord shall inherit the land. Yet a little while, and the wicked will be no more; though you look at their place, they will not be there. But the meek shall inherit the land, and delight themselves in abundant prosperity. The wicked plot against the righteous, and gnash their teeth at them; but the Lord laughs at the wicked, for he sees that their day is coming. The wicked draw the sword and bend their bows to bring down the poor and needy, to kill those who walk uprightly; their sword shall enter their own heart, and their bows shall be broken. Better is a little that the righteous person has than the abundance of many wicked. For the arms of the wicked shall be broken, but the Lord upholds the righteous. The Lord knows the days of the blameless, and their heritage will abide forever; they are not put to shame in evil times; in the days of famine they have abundance. But the wicked perish, and the enemies of the Lord are like the glory of the pastures; they vanish—like smoke they vanish away. The wicked borrow, and do not pay back, but the righteous are generous and keep giving; for those blessed by the Lord shall inherit the land, but those cursed by him shall be cut off. The

After HIS Own Heart

steps of a good man are ordered by the Lord, and he delights in his way; though he fall, he shall not be utterly cast down; for the Lord upholds him with his hand. I have been young, and now am old; yet I have not seen the righteous forsaken or their children begging bread. They are ever giving liberally and lending, and their children become a blessing. Depart from evil, and do good; so you shall abide forever. For the Lord loves justice; he will not forsake his faithful ones. The righteous shall be kept safe forever, but the children of the wicked shall be cut off. The righteous shall inherit the land, and live in it forever. The mouth of the righteous utters wisdom, and their tongue speaks justice. The law of their God is in their heart; their steps do not slip. The wicked watch for the righteous, and seek to kill them. The Lord will not abandon them to their power, or let them be condemned when they are brought to trial. Wait for the Lord, and keep to his way, and he will exalt you to inherit the land; you will look on the destruction of the wicked. I have seen the wicked oppressing, and towering like a cedar of Lebanon. Again I passed by, and they were no more; though I sought them, they could not be found. Mark the blameless, and behold the upright, for there is posterity for the peaceable. But transgressors shall be altogether destroyed; the posterity of the wicked shall be cut off. The salvation of the righteous is from the Lord; he is their stronghold in the time of trouble. The Lord helps them and rescues them; he rescues them from the wicked, and saves them, because they take refuge in him." – Psalm 37 (NRSV)

Reflection:
Psalm 37 is a meditation on the ultimate victory of the righteous over the wicked. It encourages us to trust in God's justice and sovereignty, even when the world seems unjust and the wicked seem to prosper. David urges us not to envy the wicked, but to

trust God, delight in His ways, and wait for His justice. In the midst of trouble, we are called to live righteously, avoid anger, and remain patient, trusting that God will vindicate His people in His perfect time. The psalm encourages us to look beyond the immediate and temporary prosperity of the wicked and focus on the eternal promises of God.

Trusting in God's Timing and Justice

David opens the psalm by urging us not to fret or envy those who seem to prosper through wrongdoing. We live in a world where it can seem that the wicked often get ahead, but this psalm reminds us that their success is temporary. God's justice will prevail in the end. Reflect on the times when you have seen injustice or unfairness in the world. How can you trust in God's timing and hold onto the hope that He will make all things right in the end?

Related Verses:
- **Romans 12:19** – "Beloved, never avenge yourselves, but leave it to the wrath of God, for it is written, 'Vengeance is mine, I will repay, says the Lord.'"
- **2 Peter 3:9** – "The Lord is not slow to fulfill his promise as some count slowness, but is patient toward you, not wishing that any should perish, but that all should reach repentance."

Delighting in the Lord's Will

David emphasizes the importance of taking delight in the Lord, saying, "Take delight in the Lord, and he will give you the desires of your heart." When our hearts align with God's will, our desires will naturally reflect His desires. This doesn't mean that God gives us anything we want, but that He fulfills His will and purposes in our lives. Reflect on your own desires. How can you align them more closely with God's will, trusting that His plans are best for you?

Related Verses:
- **Psalm 37:4** – "Delight yourself in the Lord, and he will give you the desires of your heart."
- **Matthew 6:33** – "But seek first the kingdom of God and his righteousness, and all these things will be added to you."

The Lord's Protection and Provision

The psalm assures us that the Lord watches over the righteous. He is our stronghold, protecting us from harm. Even when the righteous face trials or suffering, we are assured that God will deliver us. Reflect on how God has protected and provided for you, especially during times of hardship. How can you place your trust in God's protection and provision as you face challenges today?

Related Verses:
- **Psalm 121:3-4** – "He will not let your foot be moved; he who keeps you will not slumber. Behold, he who keeps Israel will neither slumber nor sleep."
- **Philippians 4:19** – "And my God will supply every need of yours according to his riches in glory in Christ Jesus."

The Fate of the Wicked

David contrasts the fate of the wicked with that of the righteous. Though the wicked seem to prosper, they will eventually be cut off, while the righteous will inherit the land and enjoy eternal security. This is a reminder that earthly success is fleeting, but God's promises to His people are eternal. Reflect on the eternal perspective this psalm gives. How does this help you persevere in faith and trust, especially when you face difficulties or witness injustice?

Related Verses:
- **Matthew 7:13-14** – "Enter by the narrow gate. For the gate is wide and the way is easy that leads to destruction, and those who enter by it are many. For the gate is narrow and the way is hard that leads to life, and those who find it are few."
- **Revelation 21:7-8** – "The one who conquers will have this heritage, and I will be his God and he will be my son. But as for the cowardly, the faithless, the detestable, as for murderers, the sexually immoral, sorcerers, idolaters, and all liars, their portion will be in the lake that burns with fire and sulfur, which is the second death."

The Call to Live with Integrity

David also calls us to live lives of integrity, turning away from evil, speaking truth, and pursuing peace. This way of living reflects our trust in God's justice and protection. Reflect on areas in your life where you may need to live more righteously. How can you commit to living with integrity and following God's ways in your daily life?

Related Verses:
- **Proverbs 12:20** – "Deceit is in the heart of those who devise evil, but those who plan peace have joy."
- **Romans 12:9** – "Let love be genuine. Abhor what is evil; hold fast to what is good."

Quote:
"God is not impressed by the strength of our weapons or the size of our armies. His protection and provision are far greater than

anything the world can offer." – Max Lucado

Application:
Psalm 37 challenges us to trust in God's timing, protection, and justice. It calls us to live with integrity, aligning our desires with God's will, and to wait patiently for His deliverance. Reflect on how you can apply these principles in your life today. How can you rejoice in God's goodness, trust in His provision, and live in a way that reflects His justice?

Prayer:
Lord, I trust in Your timing and Your justice. Help me to wait patiently for Your deliverance, knowing that Your plans are always best. I commit to delighting in You and aligning my desires with Your will. May my life reflect Your righteousness, and may I find peace in Your provision and protection. Thank You for Your faithfulness, and may I always live with integrity, trusting that You are in control. Amen.

Memorization Guide:
Step 1: Break Down the Psalm into Sections
1. **Verses 1-9**: Trusting in God's justice and timing.
2. **Verses 10-20**: The fate of the wicked and the righteous.
3. **Verses 21-31**: Living with integrity and trusting in God's protection.
4. **Verses 32-40**: The final victory of the righteous and God's salvation.

Step 2: Memorize by Key Themes and Visualizations
- **Section 1**: Trusting in God's justice (visualize God as the ultimate judge who will make all things right).

- **Section 2**: Recognizing the temporary nature of the wicked's success (visualize the fleeting nature of worldly success).
- **Section 3**: Living with integrity (visualize yourself choosing peace, speaking truth, and following God's ways).
- **Section 4**: Trusting in God's ultimate victory (visualize God's final triumph over evil and the righteous inheriting the land).

Verses:
- "Trust in the Lord, and do good; so you will live in the land, and enjoy security."
- "Take delight in the Lord, and he will give you the desires of your heart."
- "The Lord redeems the life of his servants; none of those who take refuge in him will be condemned."

Step 3: Repetition and Recitation
1. Memorize one section at a time.
2. Gradually combine the sections into the full psalm.
3. Recite the psalm daily, visualizing the key themes.

Summary of Key Images:
- Trusting in God's justice and timing.
- The temporary prosperity of the wicked vs. the eternal security of the righteous.
- Living with integrity and following God's ways.
- God's ultimate victory and deliverance for the righteous.

After HIS Own Heart

Psalm 40 – A Song of Praise for God's Deliverance

"I waited patiently for the Lord; he inclined to me and heard my cry. He drew me up from the desolate pit, out of the miry bog, and set my feet upon a rock, making my steps secure. He put a new song in my mouth, a song of praise to our God. Many will see and fear, and put their trust in the Lord. Blessed is the one who makes the Lord their trust, who does not turn to the proud, to those who go astray after false gods. You have multiplied, O Lord my God, your wondrous deeds and your thoughts toward us; none can compare with you. Were I to proclaim and tell of them, they would be more than can be counted. Sacrifice and offering you do not desire, but you have given me an open ear. Burnt offering and sin offering you have not required. Then I said, 'Here I am, I have come; in the scroll of the book it is written of me. I delight to do your will, O my God; your law is within my heart.' I have told the glad news of deliverance in the great congregation; see, I have not restrained my lips, as you know, O Lord. I have not hidden your saving help within my heart, I have spoken of your faithfulness and your salvation; I have not concealed your steadfast love and your faithfulness from the great congregation. Do not, O Lord, withhold your mercy from me; let your steadfast love and your faithfulness keep me safe forever. For evils have encompassed me without number; my iniquities have overtaken me, and I cannot see; they are more than the hairs of my head, and my heart fails me. Be pleased, O Lord, to deliver me; O Lord, make haste to help me. Let them be put to shame and confusion who seek to destroy my life; let them be turned back and brought to dishonor who desire my hurt. Let them be appalled because of their shame who say to me, 'Aha, Aha!' But may all who seek you rejoice and be glad in you; may those who love your salvation say continually, 'Great is the Lord!' As for me, I am poor and needy, but the Lord takes thought for me. You are my help and my deliverer; do not delay, O my God." – Psalm 40 (NRSV)

Reflection:

Psalm 40 is a powerful psalm of thanksgiving and trust in God's deliverance. David begins by recalling how God has lifted him out of a desperate situation, placing him on solid ground. He then praises God for His wondrous deeds, acknowledging that God's goodness is beyond measure. The psalm reveals a heart full of gratitude for God's faithfulness, a willingness to do God's will, and a desire to share His faithfulness with others. In the midst of personal struggle, David remains confident in God's ability to deliver and help him. This psalm serves as a reminder to trust in God's timing and to openly declare His goodness in our lives.

Waiting Patiently for God's Deliverance

David begins by saying, "I waited patiently for the Lord," and recounts how God responded to his cry for help. Patience in waiting is often difficult, especially when facing trials. But David's experience reminds us that when we wait on God, He hears us and acts on our behalf. Reflect on a time when you had to wait patiently for God's deliverance. How did God show up in that situation? How can you cultivate a heart that waits patiently on God, trusting in His perfect timing?

Related Verses:

- **Isaiah 40:31** – "But they who wait for the Lord shall renew their strength; they shall mount up with wings like eagles; they shall run and not be weary; they shall walk and not faint."

- **Psalm 27:14** – "Wait for the Lord; be strong, and let your heart take courage; wait for the Lord!"

God's Faithfulness and His Goodness

David praises God for His wondrous deeds and for His faithfulness to His people. He acknowledges that God's goodness is beyond measure and that His thoughts toward us are innumerable. Reflect on the goodness and faithfulness of God in your life. How has God shown His faithfulness to you in the past? How can you actively thank God for His ongoing faithfulness, even in the midst of your challenges?

Related Verses:
- **Psalm 36:5** – "Your steadfast love, O Lord, extends to the heavens, your faithfulness to the clouds."
- **Lamentations 3:22-23** – "The steadfast love of the Lord never ceases; his mercies never come to an end; they are new every morning; great is your faithfulness."

Delighting in God's Will

David declares, "I delight to do your will, O my God; your law is within my heart." This verse reflects David's deep desire to follow God's commands and live according to His will. It's a beautiful example of a heart that has been transformed by God's love and mercy. Reflect on your own heart's desires. Do you delight in doing God's will? How can you cultivate a greater desire to follow His commands and live according to His Word?

Related Verses:
- **Psalm 119:35** – "Lead me in the path of your commandments, for I delight in it."
- **Romans 12:2** – "Do not be conformed to this world, but be transformed by the renewal of your mind, that by testing you may discern what is the will of God, what is good and acceptable and perfect."

Proclaiming God's Deliverance

David expresses that he has not kept God's deliverance to himself but has proclaimed it to the great congregation. He testifies to God's faithfulness and salvation. When God delivers us, we are called to share that testimony with others. Reflect on how you can be a witness of God's goodness and deliverance in your life. How can you boldly share what God has done for you, so that others may be encouraged to trust in Him?

Related Verses:

- **Psalm 105:1** – "Oh give thanks to the Lord; call upon his name; make known his deeds among the peoples!"
- **Revelation 12:11** – "And they have conquered him by the blood of the Lamb and by the word of their testimony, for they loved not their lives even unto death."

The Lord's Help and Deliverance

David ends the psalm by crying out to God for help, declaring that God is his deliverer and that He will not delay in helping him. Even when facing overwhelming circumstances, David is confident in God's ability to rescue and protect him. Reflect on times when you have faced difficulties and how God has delivered you. How can you place your trust in God's ability to help you in your current situation, knowing that He is your deliverer?

Related Verses:

- **Psalm 18:2** – "The Lord is my rock and my fortress and my deliverer, my God, my rock, in whom I take refuge, my shield, and the horn of my salvation, my stronghold."
- **Hebrews 13:5-6** – "For he has said, 'I will never leave you nor forsake you.' So we can confidently say, 'The Lord is my helper; I will not fear; what can man do to me?'"

Quote:
"God's deliverance is not always immediate, but it is always sure. He is faithful to rescue His people in His perfect time." – Billy Graham

Application:
Psalm 40 reminds us of God's faithfulness in answering our cries for help, His goodness in delivering us from hardship, and the importance of proclaiming His salvation. Take time today to reflect on how God has delivered you and how you can proclaim His goodness to others. Whether you are in a season of waiting or deliverance, trust that God hears your prayers and will act in His perfect timing. How can you express gratitude for His faithfulness and share His goodness with others?

Prayer:
Lord, I praise You for Your faithfulness and goodness. Thank You for hearing my cry and delivering me from every trouble. I trust in Your timing and Your perfect plans for my life. Help me to delight in doing Your will and to boldly share Your deliverance with others. I place my hope and trust in You, knowing that You are my deliverer and my help. Amen.

Memorization Guide:
Step 1: Break Down the Psalm into Sections
1. **Verses 1-3**: Waiting on God and praising Him for deliverance.
2. **Verses 4-10**: Proclaiming God's goodness and delighting in His will.

3. **Verses 11-17**: Trusting in God's help and deliverance, and calling on Him for rescue.

Step 2: Memorize by Key Themes and Visualizations

- **Section 1**: Waiting and trusting in God (visualize patiently waiting for God's deliverance).
- **Section 2**: Rejoicing in God's faithfulness (visualize praising God and sharing His goodness with others).
- **Section 3**: Seeking God's help (visualize crying out to God for deliverance and trusting in His faithfulness).

Verses:

- "I waited patiently for the Lord; he inclined to me and heard my cry."
- "I delight to do your will, O my God; your law is within my heart."
- "The Lord is my help and my deliverer; do not delay, O my God."

Step 3: Repetition and Recitation

1. Memorize one section at a time.
2. Gradually combine the sections into the full psalm.
3. Recite the psalm daily, visualizing the key themes.

Summary of Key Images:

- Trusting in God's timing and deliverance.
- Rejoicing in God's goodness and proclaiming His salvation.
- Seeking God's help and deliverance in times of trouble.

Psalm 42 – Longing for God in Times of Despair

"As a deer longs for flowing streams, so my soul longs for you, O God. My soul thirsts for God, for the living God. When shall I come and behold the face of God? My tears have been my food day and night, while people say to me continually, 'Where is your God?' These things I remember, as I pour out my soul: how I went with the throng and led them in procession to the house of God, with glad shouts and songs of thanksgiving, a multitude keeping festival. Why are you cast down, O my soul, and why are you disquieted within me? Hope in God; for I shall again praise him, my help and my God. My soul is cast down within me; therefore I remember you from the land of Jordan and of Hermon, from Mount Mizar. Deep calls to deep at the thunder of your cataracts; all your waves and your billows have gone over me. By day the Lord commands his steadfast love, and at night his song is with me, a prayer to the God of my life. I say to God, my rock, 'Why have you forgotten me? Why do I go mourning because of the oppression of the enemy?' As with a deadly wound in my body, my adversaries taunt me, while they say to me continually, 'Where is your God?' Why are you cast down, O my soul, and why are you disquieted within me? Hope in God; for I shall again praise him, my help and my God." – Psalm 42 (NRSV)

Reflection:

Psalm 42 expresses a deep longing for God in the midst of personal despair. The psalmist, overwhelmed by sorrow, compares his longing for God to a thirsty deer longing for water. This psalm vividly portrays the experience of feeling distant from God and wrestling with doubts and questions, yet it also reveals the psalmist's firm trust in God's faithfulness. It invites us to express our emotions honestly before God, to bring our sorrows to Him, and to hope in His unfailing love. This psalm is a beautiful reminder that even in our deepest struggles, we can find hope and encouragement in God's presence and faithfulness.

Longing for God

The psalmist opens with the imagery of a deer longing for water, symbolizing the deep thirst of his soul for God. This longing reflects a deep desire for God's presence, especially during times of distress. When life feels overwhelming, our hearts long to experience God's peace and presence. Reflect on the areas of your life where you feel spiritually thirsty. How can you nurture a deeper longing for God, even in difficult seasons?

Related Verses:

- **Psalm 63:1** – "O God, you are my God, I seek you, my soul thirsts for you; my flesh faints for you, as in a dry and weary land where there is no water."

- **John 4:13-14** – "Jesus said to her, 'Everyone who drinks of this water will be thirsty again, but whoever drinks of the water that I will give him will never be thirsty again. The water that I will give him will become in him a spring of water welling up to eternal life.'"

A Cry for Help in the Midst of Tears

The psalmist is deeply distressed, and his tears have become his food day and night. He feels abandoned, and the mocking of others adds to his anguish. Despite this, he continues to cry out to God for help. This part of the psalm emphasizes the raw honesty that we can bring to God in our sorrow. Reflect on your own moments of sorrow. How can you bring your emotions, even your tears, before God, trusting that He hears and understands your pain?

Related Verses:
- **Psalm 56:8** – "You have kept count of my tossings; put my tears in your bottle. Are they not in your record?"
- **Revelation 21:4** – "He will wipe away every tear from their eyes, and death shall be no more, neither shall there be mourning, nor crying, nor pain anymore, for the former things have passed away."

The Call to Hope in God

In the midst of his despair, the psalmist encourages himself to "hope in God" and to wait for the day when he will again praise God. Even when emotions are overwhelming, David chooses to remind himself of God's faithfulness. This psalm teaches us the importance of preaching truth to ourselves during difficult times, particularly the truth that our hope is in God, not in our circumstances. Reflect on how you can speak words of hope and truth to yourself in times of doubt or sorrow. How can you remind yourself of God's faithfulness and promises?

Related Verses:
- **Romans 15:13** – "May the God of hope fill you with all joy and peace in believing, so that by the power of the Holy Spirit you may abound in hope."
- **Psalm 130:5** – "I wait for the Lord, my soul waits, and in his word I hope."

God's Faithfulness in the Darkness

Even when the psalmist is overwhelmed by despair, he holds on to the truth that God's love is constant. "By day the Lord commands his steadfast love, and at night his song is with me." This highlights that God's presence is with us at all times, even when we don't feel it. Reflect on how you've experienced God's faithfulness in difficult seasons. How has God shown His steadfast love, even when you were in the darkness or feeling distant from Him?

Related Verses:
- **Lamentations 3:22-23** – "The steadfast love of the Lord never ceases; his mercies never come to an end; they are new every morning; great is your faithfulness."
- **Psalm 23:4** – "Even though I walk through the valley of the shadow of death, I will fear no evil, for you are with me; your rod and your staff, they comfort me."

The Struggle with Doubt and Questions

The psalmist wrestles with doubt, questioning why God seems distant and why he must endure such suffering. "Why have you forgotten me?" is a poignant question many of us ask in times of distress. Yet, even in the midst of doubt, the psalmist resolves to hope in God's salvation. It is important to bring our questions and doubts before God, trusting that He will answer us in His perfect time. Reflect on your own struggles with doubt or unanswered questions. How can you bring your doubts to God, trusting that He will guide you and bring you peace?

Related Verses:
- **Habakkuk 1:2** – "O Lord, how long shall I cry for help, and you will not hear? Or cry to you 'Violence!' and you will not save?"
- **James 1:5** – "If any of you lacks wisdom, let him ask of God, who gives generously to all without reproach, and it will be given him."

Trusting in God's Salvation

David closes the psalm with a confident declaration of hope: "For I shall again praise him, my help and my God." Despite the pain and doubt, David knows that God will deliver him. This ultimate trust in God's salvation, even in the midst of suffering, provides a powerful reminder that God is faithful to deliver us from despair. Reflect on how you can cultivate a heart that trusts God's ultimate salvation, even when you can't see the way forward. How can you hold on to hope in the midst of your struggles, knowing that God's deliverance is coming?

Related Verses:
- **Romans 8:24-25** – "For in this hope we were saved. Now hope that is seen is not hope. For who hopes for what he sees? But if we hope for what we do not see, we wait for it with patience."
- **Psalm 18:2** – "The Lord is my rock and my fortress and my deliverer, my God, my rock, in whom I take refuge, my shield, and the horn of my salvation, my stronghold."

Quote:
"Hope is not a passive waiting, but an active trusting in God's timing and promises, even in the midst of life's most difficult seasons." – Elisabeth Elliot

Application:
Psalm 42 encourages us to express our honest emotions before God, even in our darkest moments. It calls us to trust in God's faithfulness, to wait patiently for His deliverance, and to hold on to hope in the midst of despair. Take time today to reflect on your own emotional and spiritual journey. How can you be more honest with God about your struggles? How can you actively choose to hope in Him, even when you feel overwhelmed or distant from Him?

Prayer:

Lord, my soul longs for You, and my heart thirsts for Your presence. In times of despair, when I feel far from You, help me to remember Your faithfulness and to trust in Your deliverance. Even in the darkness, may I find comfort in Your steadfast love and Your promises. Help me to hope in You, knowing that You will never forsake me. I trust in Your salvation, and I will praise You, my help and my God. Amen.

Memorization Guide:
Step 1: Break Down the Psalm into Sections
1. **Verses 1-5**: Longing for God and expressing sorrow.
2. **Verses 6-10**: Trusting in God's love, despite doubts and struggles.
3. **Verses 11-12**: Reaffirming hope and trust in God's deliverance.

Step 2: Memorize by Key Themes and Visualizations
- **Section 1**: Longing for God's presence (visualize thirsting for God as a deer thirsts for water).
- **Section 2**: Trusting God in the midst of doubt (visualize God's love surrounding you, even in the darkest moments).
- **Section 3**: Reaffirming hope in God's salvation (visualize yourself confidently praising God in the midst of struggle).

Verses:
- "As a deer longs for flowing streams, so my soul longs for you, O God."

- "Why are you cast down, O my soul, and why are you disquieted within me? Hope in God; for I shall again praise him, my help and my God."
- "By day the Lord commands his steadfast love, and at night his song is with me, a prayer to the God of my life."

Step 3: Repetition and Recitation

1. Memorize one section at a time.
2. Gradually combine the sections into the full psalm.
3. Recite the psalm daily, visualizing the key themes.

Summary of Key Images:

- Thirsting for God's presence.
- Trusting in God's love during times of doubt.
- Confidently praising God, knowing His deliverance is coming.

Psalm 46 – God is Our Refuge and Strength

"God is our refuge and strength, a very present help in trouble. Therefore we will not fear, though the earth should change, though the mountains shake in the heart of the sea; though its waters roar and foam, though the mountains tremble with its tumult. Selah. There is a river whose streams make glad the city of God, the holy habitation of the Most High. God is in the midst of her; she shall not be moved; God will help her when the morning dawns. The nations are in an uproar, the kingdoms totter; he utters his voice, the earth melts. The Lord of hosts is with us; the God of Jacob is our refuge. Selah. Come, behold the works of the Lord; see what desolations he has brought on the earth. He makes wars cease to the end of the earth; he breaks the bow, and shatters the spear; he burns the shields with fire. 'Be still, and know that I am God. I am exalted among the nations, I am exalted in the earth.' The Lord of hosts is with us; the God of Jacob is our refuge. Selah." – Psalm 46 (NRSV)

Reflection:

Psalm 46 is a powerful reminder of God's sovereignty, protection, and presence in times of turmoil. The psalmist speaks of a world that may be shaking, with natural disasters and nations in conflict, but even in the midst of chaos, God is a refuge and a source of strength. The imagery of God as a refuge, and the declaration that "God is our refuge and strength," invites us to take refuge in Him, trust His presence, and experience peace amid life's storms. This psalm calls us to be still and trust in God's control, knowing that He is with us, sovereign over all.

God as Our Refuge and Strength

The psalm begins with the powerful declaration that "God is our refuge and strength, a very present help in trouble." No matter what happens in the world, God is always present and ready to protect us. He is our safe place, our shelter in the storm. Reflect on the ways that God has been a refuge in your life. In moments of difficulty or fear, how can you turn to Him as your ultimate place of safety and strength?

Related Verses:

- **Psalm 62:7-8** – "On God rests my salvation and my glory; my mighty rock, my refuge is God. Trust in him at all times, O people; pour out your heart before him; God is a refuge for us."

- **Isaiah 41:10** – "Fear not, for I am with you; be not dismayed, for I am your God; I will strengthen you, I will help you, I will uphold you with my righteous right hand."

Fearless in the Midst of Chaos

The psalmist paints a dramatic picture of the earth shaking, mountains trembling, and waters roaring. In the midst of such chaos, the psalmist declares, "Therefore we will not fear." This assurance of peace in the midst of turmoil is not because of the absence of problems, but because of the presence of God. Reflect on times when you've faced uncertainty or chaos in your life. How did you experience God's peace in those moments, and how can you continue to trust Him when life feels unstable?

Related Verses:

- **Philippians 4:6-7** – "Do not be anxious about anything, but in everything by prayer and supplication with thanksgiving let your requests be made known to God. And the peace of God, which surpasses all understanding, will guard your hearts and your minds in Christ Jesus."

- **Isaiah 26:3** – "You keep him in perfect peace whose mind is stayed on you, because he trusts in you."

The River of God's Presence

There is a beautiful image in this psalm of a river whose streams make glad the city of God. The river symbolizes God's presence, flowing through His people and providing joy and sustenance. Even in the midst of turbulent times, the psalmist is assured that God's presence brings peace and gladness. Reflect on how God's presence has been like a river in your own life, bringing refreshment and peace. How can you cultivate a deeper awareness of God's presence in your life, especially in times of trouble?

Related Verses:
- **John 7:38** – "Whoever believes in me, as the Scripture has said, 'Out of his heart will flow rivers of living water.'"
- **Revelation 22:1-2** – "Then the angel showed me the river of the water of life, bright as crystal, flowing from the throne of God and of the Lamb..."

God's Sovereignty Over the Nations

The psalmist acknowledges that the nations are in turmoil, but God speaks, and the earth melts. This is a reminder that, despite the political unrest and the power of earthly kingdoms, God remains sovereign and in control of all things. Reflect on how God's sovereignty provides comfort in a world filled with instability. When you face situations that seem out of control, how can you trust that God is still in charge and working His purposes?

Related Verses:
- **Psalm 2:4** – "He who sits in the heavens laughs; the Lord holds them in derision."

- **Revelation 19:6** – "Then I heard what seemed to be the voice of a great multitude, like the roar of many waters and like the sound of mighty peals of thunder, crying out, 'Hallelujah! For the Lord our God the Almighty reigns.'"

Be Still and Know That I Am God

One of the most famous verses in Psalm 46 is "Be still, and know that I am God." In the midst of noise, distractions, and uncertainty, God calls us to be still and recognize His sovereignty. In the stillness, we are reminded that God is in control, and we can rest in His power and presence. Reflect on how you can be still before God in your own life. How can you create space for silence and stillness to hear God's voice, trust His promises, and experience His peace?

Related Verses:
- **Exodus 14:14** – "The Lord will fight for you, and you have only to be silent."
- **Psalm 37:7** – "Be still before the Lord and wait patiently for him; fret not yourself over the one who prospers in his way, over the man who carries out evil devices."

The Lord of Hosts is With Us

The psalm concludes by repeating the truth that "The Lord of hosts is with us; the God of Jacob is our refuge." This declaration reinforces the reality that God is present with His people and that He is our protector. The psalmist is confident in God's power and presence. Reflect on how God's presence as "the Lord of hosts" (the Lord of angel armies) provides you with confidence and peace. How can you rely on God's presence in your life, knowing that He fights on your behalf?

Related Verses:

- **Psalm 118:6** – "The Lord is on my side; I will not fear. What can man do to me?"
- **Romans 8:31** – "What then shall we say to these things? If God is for us, who can be against us?"

Quote:
"In times of crisis, we can find peace not in the absence of problems but in the presence of God." – Tim Keller

Application:
Psalm 46 calls us to trust in God's sovereignty, find refuge in His presence, and be still before Him. Reflect on your current circumstances and how you can find peace by trusting in God's control over everything. Are you facing uncertainty or challenges today? Take time to be still before God and remind yourself that He is with you, your refuge and strength, a very present help in trouble. How can you live with the confidence that God is in control and that His presence is your source of peace?

Prayer:
Lord, I thank You for being my refuge and strength. In the midst of chaos and uncertainty, I choose to trust in Your sovereignty and find peace in Your presence. Help me to be still and know that You are God, exalted over all things. Thank You for being with me in every circumstance, providing me with strength and security. I will rest in Your protection, knowing that You are my refuge. Amen.

Memorization Guide:
Step 1: Break Down the Psalm into Sections

1. **Verses 1-3**: God is our refuge and strength; we will not fear.
2. **Verses 4-7**: The river of God's presence and God's sovereignty over the nations.
3. **Verses 8-11**: Be still and know that God is in control; the Lord of hosts is with us.

Step 2: Memorize by Key Themes and Visualizations

- **Section 1**: Trusting in God as our refuge (visualize finding shelter in God's presence).
- **Section 2**: Rejoicing in God's presence and sovereignty (visualize the river of life flowing through you).
- **Section 3**: Being still and trusting in God's control (visualize quieting your heart before God).

Verses:

- "God is our refuge and strength, a very present help in trouble."
- "Be still, and know that I am God."
- "The Lord of hosts is with us; the God of Jacob is our refuge."

Step 3: Repetition and Recitation

1. Memorize one section at a time.
2. Gradually combine the sections into the full psalm.
3. Recite the psalm daily, visualizing the key themes.

Summary of Key Images:

- God as our refuge and strength in times of trouble.

- The river of God's presence bringing peace and gladness.
- Being still and trusting in God's sovereignty.

Psalm 47 – God's Sovereignty and Universal Kingship

"Clap your hands, all you peoples; shout to God with loud songs of joy. For the Lord, the Most High, is awesome, the great king over all the earth. He subdued peoples under us, and nations under our feet. He chose our heritage for us, the pride of Jacob whom he loves. Selah. God has gone up with a shout, the Lord with the sound of a trumpet. Sing praises to God, sing praises; sing praises to our King, sing praises. For God is the king of all the earth; sing praises with a psalm. God reigns over the nations; God sits on his holy throne. The princes of the peoples gather as the people of the God of Abraham. For the shields of the earth belong to God; he is highly exalted." – Psalm 47 (NRSV)

Reflection:

Psalm 47 is a psalm of praise and exaltation, calling all peoples to recognize God's sovereignty over the earth. It celebrates the kingship of God, who reigns over all nations and peoples. The psalmist calls for joyful praise, acknowledging that God is not only the King of Israel but the King of the entire world. This psalm invites us to rejoice in the power of God, remembering that He is the ruler of the nations and the one who holds the entire world in His hands. We are called to worship God with joy, recognizing His greatness and sovereignty.

Clapping Hands and Shouting for Joy

The psalm begins with a call to action: "Clap your hands, all you peoples; shout to God with loud songs of joy." This is an invitation to participate in enthusiastic and public praise for God's greatness. Praise is not meant to be passive but an active expression of joy and gratitude. Reflect on how you express your praise to God. How can you approach worship with a heart full of joy and an active desire to honor Him?

Related Verses:
- **Psalm 98:4** – "Make a joyful noise to the Lord, all the earth; break forth into joyous song and sing praises."
- **Psalm 100:1-2** – "Make a joyful noise to the Lord, all the earth. Serve the Lord with gladness! Come into his presence with singing!"

God as the Great King Over All the Earth

The psalmist praises God as the "great king over all the earth." His reign extends beyond Israel and encompasses every nation. This declaration challenges us to see God as the supreme ruler over everything, not just our personal lives, but over the entire world. Reflect on how recognizing God's sovereignty over all the earth changes your perspective on the world and your own circumstances. How can this reminder help you trust God's control over all things, especially in times of uncertainty?

Related Verses:
- **1 Chronicles 29:11** – "Yours, O Lord, is the greatness and the power and the glory and the victory and the majesty, for all that is in the heavens and in the earth is yours. Yours is the kingdom, O Lord, and you are exalted as head above all."
- **Revelation 11:15** – "Then the seventh angel blew his trumpet, and there were loud voices in heaven, saying, 'The kingdom of the world has become the kingdom of our Lord and of his Christ, and he shall reign forever and ever.'"

God's Victory Over Nations

The psalm speaks of God's power to subdue nations and peoples. God's victory is complete and sovereign, and He establishes His people in the land He has chosen for them. The imagery of God going up with a shout, the sound of a trumpet, and singing praises to Him emphasizes the greatness of God's reign. This victory is not just historical but a present reality. Reflect on how God's sovereignty brings victory into your life. How can you trust in His power to bring victory over struggles, battles, or challenges you face today?

Related Verses:
- **Psalm 24:8-10** – "Who is this King of glory? The Lord, strong and mighty, the Lord, mighty in battle!"
- **Isaiah 40:10** – "Behold, the Lord God comes with might, and his arm rules for him; behold, his reward is with him, and his recompense before him."

Sing Praises to God, Our King

The psalmist calls for repeated praise to God, saying, "Sing praises to God, sing praises; sing praises to our King, sing praises." This is a call to joyful worship and adoration, acknowledging God's kingship over all the earth. Reflect on how you can deepen your personal worship and praise of God. How can you cultivate a heart that continually praises God, not just in church but in everyday moments?

Related Verses:
- **Psalm 145:1-2** – "I will extol you, my God and King, and bless your name forever and ever. Every day I will bless you and praise your name forever and ever."
- **Colossians 3:16** – "Let the word of Christ dwell in you richly, teaching and admonishing one another in all wisdom, singing psalms and hymns and spiritual songs, with thankfulness in your hearts to God."

God's Sovereign Rule Over the Nations

The psalmist affirms that God reigns over all the nations and that the peoples of the earth belong to Him. The "princes of the peoples" are gathered before God, acknowledging that He is the ruler of the earth. This truth reminds us that God is in control of history and the world's political systems, even when it appears that things are out of control. Reflect on how God's sovereignty gives you peace, especially when the world feels chaotic or uncertain. How can you rest in the assurance that God reigns over all?

Related Verses:

- **Psalm 22:28** – "For kingship belongs to the Lord, and he rules over the nations."

- **Daniel 2:21** – "He changes times and seasons; he removes kings and sets up kings; he gives wisdom to the wise and knowledge to those who have understanding."

The Lord of Hosts is With Us

The psalmist concludes by declaring that "the Lord of hosts is with us; the God of Jacob is our refuge." This reinforces the confidence that, no matter the circumstances, God is with His people and will protect them. The "Lord of hosts" refers to God's power over all the heavenly armies, and this assures us that He is always fighting for us. Reflect on the security you find in knowing that the Lord of hosts is with you. How does this truth give you courage to face challenges, knowing that God is always by your side?

Related Verses:

- **Psalm 118:6** – "The Lord is on my side; I will not fear. What can man do to me?"

- **Romans 8:31** – "What then shall we say to these things? If God is for us, who can be against us?"

Quote:
"God's sovereignty over all the nations is not only a source of our peace but also a call to action, to live with the confidence that God reigns over every situation in our lives." – John Piper

Application:
Psalm 47 calls us to rejoice in God's sovereignty and power. It encourages us to praise God for His reign over all the earth, trusting that He is in control of every situation. Reflect on areas of your life where you need to acknowledge God's sovereignty. How can you respond to the truth that God is the King of all the earth by living with joy, peace, and confidence in His control?

Prayer:
Lord, You are the great King over all the earth. I praise You for Your sovereign rule, and I trust in Your power and control over every aspect of my life. Thank You for being with me, for being my refuge and strength. Help me to live with confidence in Your sovereignty, knowing that You are in control of all things. I will continue to praise You, my King, with joy and thanksgiving. Amen.

Memorization Guide:
Step 1: Break Down the Psalm into Sections

1. **Verses 1-4**: A call to praise and recognition of God's kingship.
2. **Verses 5-7**: God's sovereignty over the nations and His call for praise.
3. **Verses 8-9**: The Lord of hosts is with us and our refuge.

Step 2: Memorize by Key Themes and Visualizations
- **Section 1**: Praising God as King (visualize lifting your hands in praise to God as the King).
- **Section 2**: Rejoicing in God's sovereignty (visualize God reigning over all the nations).
- **Section 3**: Trusting in God's protection (visualize God's presence as your refuge and strength).

Verses:
- "Clap your hands, all you peoples; shout to God with loud songs of joy."
- "For God is the king of all the earth; sing praises with a psalm."
- "The Lord of hosts is with us; the God of Jacob is our refuge."

Step 3: Repetition and Recitation
1. Memorize one section at a time.
2. Gradually combine the sections into the full psalm.
3. Recite the psalm daily, visualizing the key themes.

Summary of Key Images:
- Praising God as the King over all the earth.
- Rejoicing in God's sovereignty and control over the nations.
- Trusting in God's protection and presence as our refuge.

Psalm 49 – The Futility of Trusting in Wealth

"Hear this, all you peoples; give ear, all inhabitants of the world, both low and high, rich and poor together. My mouth shall speak wisdom; the meditation of my heart shall be understanding. I will incline my ear to a proverb; I will solve my riddle to the music of the lyre. Why should I fear in times of trouble, when the iniquity of my persecutors surrounds me, those who trust in their wealth and boast of the abundance of their riches? Truly, no man can ransom another, or give to God the price of his life, for the ransom of life is costly, and can never suffice, that he should live on forever and never see the pit. For he sees that even the wise die; the fool and the stupid alike must perish and leave their wealth to others. Their graves are their homes forever, their dwelling places to all generations, though they named lands their own. Man cannot abide in his pomp; he is like the beasts that perish. This is the fate of those who have foolish confidence, the end of those who are pleased with their portion. Selah. Like sheep they are appointed for Sheol; death shall be their shepherd; and the upright shall rule over them in the morning. Their form shall be consumed in Sheol, with no place to dwell. But God will ransom my soul from the power of Sheol, for he will receive me. Selah. Be not afraid when a man becomes rich, when the glory of his house increases. For when he dies he will carry nothing away; his glory will not go down after him. For though, while he lives, he counts himself blessed—and though you get praise when you do well for yourself—his soul will go to the generation of his fathers, who will never again see the light. Man in his pomp yet without understanding is like the beasts that perish." – Psalm 49 (NRSV)

Reflection:

Psalm 49 is a sobering reflection on the futility of trusting in wealth and material success. The psalmist reminds us that, despite our achievements and accumulation of wealth, we cannot escape the inevitability of death. Wealth, power, and status do not offer true security. The psalm emphasizes that, in the end, all will face death, and we cannot purchase our way out of it. True security comes not from material wealth, but from placing our trust in God, who alone can ransom our souls and offer us eternal life. This psalm calls us to examine where we place our trust and to focus on eternal, rather than temporary, riches.

The Futility of Wealth
The psalm begins with a reflection on the temporary nature of wealth. The psalmist contrasts those who trust in their wealth and boast in their riches with the reality that no one can ransom their life from death. Reflect on how you view wealth in your life. Do you place your trust in material things, or do you recognize that true security comes from God alone? How can you shift your focus from temporary wealth to eternal treasures?

Related Verses:
- **Matthew 6:19-21** – "Do not lay up for yourselves treasures on earth, where moth and rust destroy and where thieves break in and steal, but lay up for yourselves treasures in heaven, where neither moth nor rust destroys and where thieves do not break in and steal. For where your treasure is, there your heart will be also."
- **Luke 12:15** – "And he said to them, 'Take care, and be on your guard against all covetousness, for one's life does not consist in the abundance of his possessions.'"

Death is the Great Equalizer
The psalmist makes it clear that death comes for all, whether rich

or poor, wise or foolish. Death is the great equalizer, and no one can escape it, no matter their wealth or status. Reflect on how the inevitability of death changes your perspective on life. How does it help you prioritize what is truly important? Are there areas where you need to focus more on eternal matters, such as your relationship with God, than on temporary achievements?

Related Verses:
- **Ecclesiastes 3:19-20** – "For what happens to the children of man happens to animals; as one dies, so dies the other. They all have the same breath, and man has no advantage over the animals, for all is vanity. All go to one place. All are from the dust, and to dust all return."
- **1 Timothy 6:7** – "For we brought nothing into the world, and we cannot take anything out of the world."

God's Ransom for the Soul

The psalmist contrasts the fate of those who trust in wealth with the promise that God will ransom the soul of the righteous. While material wealth cannot save us, God alone can redeem us from the power of death and Sheol. Reflect on the assurance that, though wealth is fleeting, God's redemption is eternal. How does knowing that God has ransomed your soul through Christ affect the way you live today? How can you live with an eternal perspective, knowing that God's love and redemption are far more valuable than any earthly wealth?

Related Verses:
- **Mark 8:36** – "For what does it profit a man to gain the whole world and forfeit his soul?"
- **Psalm 103:4** – "Who redeems your life from the pit, who crowns you with steadfast love and mercy."

Don't Be Afraid of the Rich

In the final verses of the psalm, the psalmist encourages us not to fear or envy the rich, for they will not take their wealth with them when they die. Their glory will not follow them, and their wealth cannot save them from death. Reflect on your own attitudes toward wealth and success. Are you tempted to envy those who seem to have it all? How can you find contentment and peace in knowing that God, not wealth, is the true source of security?

Related Verses:
- **Proverbs 23:4-5** – "Do not toil to acquire wealth; be discerning enough to desist. When your eyes light on it, it is gone, for suddenly it sprouts wings, flying like an eagle toward heaven."
- **Matthew 19:23-24** – "And Jesus said to his disciples, 'Truly, I say to you, it will be hard for a rich person to enter the kingdom of heaven. Again I tell you, it is easier for a camel to go through the eye of a needle than for a rich person to enter the kingdom of God.'"

Quote:
"The greatest use of wealth is to serve others and to invest in what lasts for eternity, not in what will soon pass away." – Randy Alcorn

---

Application:
Psalm 49 calls us to reflect on the futility of trusting in wealth and reminds us that true security comes only from God. Take time today to reflect on where your security lies. Are there areas where you are tempted to place your trust in temporary things—wealth, success, or possessions? How can you focus on eternal treasures, such as your relationship with God, loving others, and investing in the Kingdom of God?

Prayer:

Lord, thank You for the reminder that true security is found in You, not in wealth or possessions. Help me to place my trust in Your eternal promises rather than in the fleeting things of this world. I recognize that wealth cannot save me, but You, Lord, have redeemed my soul. I choose to live with an eternal perspective, focusing on the things that truly matter. Guide me to use what You've given me to honor You and bless others. Amen.

Memorization Guide:
Step 1: Break Down the Psalm into Sections

1. **Verses 1-4**: A call to listen and reflect on the futility of wealth.

2. **Verses 5-9**: The temporary nature of wealth and the inevitability of death.

3. **Verses 10-12**: The fate of the rich and the hope of redemption in God.

4. **Verses 13-20**: Don't fear the wealthy; trust in God's eternal redemption.

Step 2: Memorize by Key Themes and Visualizations

- **Section 1**: Reflecting on the futility of wealth (visualize the temporary nature of riches).

- **Section 2**: The equality of death for all (visualize the graves of the rich and the poor side by side).

- **Section 3**: God's redemption (visualize God rescuing your soul from death).

- **Section 4**: Trusting in God, not wealth (visualize yourself living with eternal perspective).

Verses:
- "Why should I fear in times of trouble, when the iniquity of my persecutors surrounds me?"
- "Truly, no man can ransom another, or give to God the price of his life."
- "But God will ransom my soul from the power of Sheol, for he will receive me."
- "For though, while he lives, he counts himself blessed... his soul will go to the generation of his fathers."

Step 3: Repetition and Recitation
1. Memorize one section at a time.
2. Gradually combine the sections into the full psalm.
3. Recite the psalm daily, visualizing the key themes.

Summary of Key Images:
- The fleeting nature of wealth and the certainty of death.
- God as the Redeemer who ransoms our souls.
- The futility of envying the rich and the eternal security found in God.

After HIS Own Heart

Psalm 51 – A Prayer of Repentance and Restoration

"Have mercy on me, O God, according to your steadfast love; according to your abundant mercy blot out my transgressions. Wash me thoroughly from my iniquity, and cleanse me from my sin. For I know my transgressions, and my sin is ever before me. Against you, you alone, have I sinned and done what is evil in your sight, so that you are justified in your sentence and blameless when you pass judgment. Indeed, I was born guilty, a sinner when my mother conceived me. You desire truth in the inward being; therefore teach me wisdom in my secret heart. Purge me with hyssop, and I shall be clean; wash me, and I shall be whiter than snow. Let me hear joy and gladness; let the bones that you have crushed rejoice. Hide your face from my sins, and blot out all my iniquities. Create in me a clean heart, O God, and put a new and right spirit within me. Do not cast me away from your presence, and do not take your holy spirit from me. Restore to me the joy of your salvation, and sustain in me a willing spirit. Then I will teach transgressors your ways, and sinners will return to you. Deliver me from bloodshed, O God, O God of my salvation, and my tongue will sing aloud of your deliverance. O Lord, open my lips, and my mouth will declare your praise. For you have no delight in sacrifice; if I were to give a burnt offering, you would not be pleased. The sacrifice acceptable to God is a broken spirit; a broken and contrite heart, O God, you will not despise. Do good to Zion in your good pleasure; rebuild the walls of Jerusalem; then you will delight in right sacrifices, in burnt offerings and whole burnt offerings; then bulls will be offered on your altar." – Psalm 51 (NRSV)

Reflection:

Psalm 51 is one of the most powerful prayers of repentance in the Bible, written by King David after his sin with Bathsheba and the murder of her husband, Uriah. In this psalm, David acknowledges his sin, confesses his transgressions, and asks God for mercy, forgiveness, and restoration. The psalm is a deep reflection on the nature of sin, the need for repentance, and the grace of God to cleanse and renew the heart. It highlights the importance of inward transformation, not just outward ritual, and calls for a humble and contrite heart. This psalm invites us to come before God honestly, confessing our sins and seeking His forgiveness and restoration.

A Cry for Mercy

David begins the psalm by pleading for God's mercy, appealing to God's steadfast love and abundant mercy. In his time of sin, David knew that he could not rely on his own goodness but on God's grace and compassion. Reflect on your own need for God's mercy. Have you ever felt the weight of your sin and been overwhelmed by the need for God's forgiveness? How can you approach God today with a heart that recognizes His mercy as the only source of hope and restoration?

Related Verses:

- **Ephesians 2:4-5** – "But God, being rich in mercy, because of the great love with which he loved us, even when we were dead in our trespasses, made us alive together with Christ—by grace you have been saved."

- **1 John 1:9** – "If we confess our sins, he is faithful and just to forgive us our sins and to cleanse us from all unrighteousness."

Confession of Sin

David acknowledges that his sin is ever before him and that it is ultimately against God. He recognizes that sin is not just a violation of human relationships, but a direct offense against God's holiness. Reflect on the importance of acknowledging sin in your own life, not just in the context of how it affects others, but in how it grieves God's heart. How can you be more honest with yourself and with God about the sin that needs to be confessed and repented of?

Related Verses:
- **Psalm 32:5** – "I acknowledged my sin to you, and I did not hide my iniquity; I said, 'I will confess my transgressions to the Lord,' and you forgave the guilt of my sin."
- **Romans 3:23** – "For all have sinned and fall short of the glory of God."

The Desire for Inward Transformation

David expresses the need for inward transformation, asking God to create a clean heart in him. He understands that true repentance goes beyond external actions or rituals; it involves a changed heart and spirit. Reflect on areas of your life where you may need God to transform your heart. Is there any sin that you need God to purify in your thoughts, attitudes, or desires? How can you invite God to bring about lasting change in you, rather than merely changing your outward behavior?

Related Verses:
- **2 Corinthians 5:17** – "Therefore, if anyone is in Christ, he is a new creation. The old has passed away; behold, the new has come."
- **Ezekiel 36:26** – "And I will give you a new heart, and a new spirit I will put within you. And I will remove the heart of stone from your flesh and give you a heart of flesh."

The Call for Joy and Restoration

David desires to experience the joy of God's salvation once

again. His sin has caused a loss of joy, but he asks God to restore it to him. True repentance leads to restoration, and the psalmist longs to experience the peace and joy that come with being in right relationship with God. Reflect on the joy of salvation and the peace that comes from knowing you are forgiven. Have you experienced God's restoring grace in your life? How can you restore the joy of your salvation, even in difficult seasons?

Related Verses:
- **Psalm 51:12** – "Restore to me the joy of your salvation, and uphold me with a willing spirit."
- **Nehemiah 8:10** – "Do not grieve, for the joy of the Lord is your strength."

The True Sacrifice: A Broken and Contrite Heart

David recognizes that God desires a broken and contrite heart more than external sacrifices. God is not pleased with ritualistic offerings if the heart is not repentant. Reflect on the significance of a humble and contrite heart before God. How can you approach God not just with actions but with an attitude of humility, brokenness, and sincerity in repentance?

Related Verses:
- **Isaiah 66:2** – "All these things my hand has made, and so all these things came to be, declares the Lord. But this is the one to whom I will look: he who is humble and contrite in spirit and trembles at my word."
- **Micah 6:6-8** – "With what shall I come before the Lord, and bow myself before God on high? Shall I come before him with burnt offerings, with calves a year old? He has told you, O man, what is good; and what does the Lord require of you but to do justice, and to love kindness, and to walk humbly with your God?"

After HIS Own Heart

Quote:
"Repentance is not about feeling bad about the past but about living differently in the present and future because of the grace of God." – Tim Keller

Application:
Psalm 51 is a powerful reminder of the importance of repentance and the depth of God's mercy. Take time today to reflect on your own heart. Is there sin that needs to be confessed? Are there areas where you need God to create in you a clean heart and restore the joy of His salvation? Remember that God is faithful to forgive and to restore, and His mercy is always greater than our failures. Seek His cleansing today, and allow His love to transform you inwardly and outwardly.

Prayer:
Lord, I come to You with a humble heart, asking for Your mercy and forgiveness. Cleanse me from my sin and restore to me the joy of Your salvation. Create in me a clean heart, O God, and renew a right spirit within me. Help me to walk in humility and repentance, always seeking Your will. Thank You for Your steadfast love and grace that forgive and heal. May I continually experience the joy and peace that come from being reconciled to You. Amen.

Memorization Guide:
Step 1: Break Down the Psalm into Sections
1. **Verses 1-6**: A cry for mercy and acknowledgment of sin.
2. **Verses 7-12**: A prayer for cleansing, restoration, and renewal.

3. **Verses 13-19**: The call to teach others and the true sacrifice of a contrite heart.

Step 2: Memorize by Key Themes and Visualizations
- **Section 1**: Acknowledging sin and asking for mercy (visualize a heart in need of God's cleansing).
- **Section 2**: Seeking transformation and restoration (visualize God creating a clean heart within you).
- **Section 3**: Living with a contrite heart (visualize offering your brokenness to God as your true sacrifice).

Verses:
- "Have mercy on me, O God, according to your steadfast love."
- "Create in me a clean heart, O God, and put a new and right spirit within me."
- "The sacrifice acceptable to God is a broken spirit; a broken and contrite heart, O God, you will not despise."

Step 3: Repetition and Recitation
1. Memorize one section at a time.
2. Gradually combine the sections into the full psalm.
3. Recite the psalm daily, visualizing the key themes.

Summary of Key Images:
- A cry for mercy and forgiveness.
- A clean heart and renewed spirit created by God.
- A broken and contrite heart as the true sacrifice.

After HIS Own Heart

Psalm 56 – Trusting God When Afraid

"Be gracious to me, O God, for people trample on me; all day long foes oppress me; my enemies trample on me all day long, for many fight against me. O Most High, when I am afraid, I put my trust in you. In God, whose word I praise, in God I trust; I am not afraid; what can flesh do to me? All day long they seek to injure my cause; all their thoughts are against me for evil. They stir up strife, they lurk, they watch my steps. As they hope to have my life, so repay them for their wickedness; in wrath cast down the peoples, O God. You have kept count of my tossings; put my tears in your bottle. Are they not in your record? Then my enemies will retreat on the day when I call. This I know, that God is for me. In God, whose word I praise, in the Lord, whose word I praise, in God I trust; I am not afraid; what can man do to me? I am bound by vows to you, O God; I will offer to you thank offerings. For you have delivered my soul from death, and my feet from falling, so that I may walk before God in the light of life." – Psalm 56 (NRSV)

Reflection:

Psalm 56 is a psalm of trust and hope in God, written by David when he was captured by the Philistines in Gath. In the face of fear, David cries out to God for mercy and help, expressing both his anxiety and his deep trust in God's protection. Despite his circumstances, David refuses to give in to fear, confidently declaring that God is his refuge and deliverer. This psalm teaches us how to respond to fear with faith, to rely on God's promises, and to remember that He is always with us, even in our darkest moments.

A Cry for God's Mercy in Times of Fear

David begins the psalm with a plea for mercy, acknowledging the fear he feels because of the oppression he faces. Fear is a natural response to danger, but David chooses to seek refuge in God rather than succumb to anxiety. Reflect on your own fears. What are the circumstances in your life that make you feel afraid? How can you bring your fears before God, trusting in His mercy and protection?

Related Verses:

- **Psalm 34:4** – "I sought the Lord, and he answered me and delivered me from all my fears."
- **Isaiah 41:10** – "Fear not, for I am with you; be not dismayed, for I am your God; I will strengthen you, I will help you, I will uphold you with my righteous right hand."

Trusting in God When Afraid

One of the most powerful verses in Psalm 56 is when David declares, "When I am afraid, I put my trust in you." Fear often leads us to question our safety, but David shows us that in the face of fear, we can choose to trust God. Trusting God in our fear doesn't mean we are without fear, but that we acknowledge God's sovereignty over our circumstances. Reflect on the areas in your life where fear holds sway. How can you choose to trust God with those fears, knowing that He is greater than anything we face?

Related Verses:

- **Proverbs 3:5-6** – "Trust in the Lord with all your heart, and do not lean on your own understanding. In all your ways acknowledge him, and he will make straight your paths."
- **2 Timothy 1:7** – "For God gave us a spirit not of fear but of power and love and self-control."

God Keeps Count of Our Tears

David acknowledges that God sees and values his suffering, saying, "You have kept count of my tossings; put my tears in your bottle." This verse is a beautiful picture of God's intimate care for His people. He sees our pain, collects our tears, and remembers every hardship we face. Reflect on how God has cared for you in your moments of difficulty. Have you ever experienced His comfort in ways that reminded you of His deep concern for your life?

Related Verses:
- **Psalm 34:18** – "The Lord is near to the brokenhearted and saves the crushed in spirit."
- **Revelation 21:4** – "He will wipe away every tear from their eyes, and death shall be no more, neither shall there be mourning, nor crying, nor pain anymore, for the former things have passed away."

Confidence in God's Protection

In the midst of his fears, David expresses confidence in God's protection, saying, "This I know, that God is for me." This bold statement reflects David's unwavering trust in God's presence and faithfulness. No matter what his enemies may do, David knows that God is on his side. Reflect on the ways God has been for you in your life. How can you stand firm in the assurance that God is for you, even when facing difficulties or opposition?

Related Verses:
- **Romans 8:31** – "What then shall we say to these things? If God is for us, who can be against us?"
- **Psalm 118:6** – "The Lord is on my side; I will not fear. What can man do to me?"

Living with a Heart of Gratitude

David ends the psalm by declaring his commitment to thank God for His deliverance. He promises to offer thanks to God for the ways He has rescued him. Gratitude is a powerful antidote to fear. When we focus on God's faithfulness and the ways He has delivered us, our hearts are filled with peace and trust. Reflect on the ways God has delivered you in the past. How can you cultivate a heart of gratitude, even when facing current challenges?

Related Verses:

- **Psalm 107:1** – "Oh give thanks to the Lord, for he is good, for his steadfast love endures forever."
- **Colossians 3:15** – "And let the peace of Christ rule in your hearts, to which indeed you were called in one body. And be thankful."

Quote:

"Faith does not eliminate fear. It just puts it in its proper place." – Max Lucado

---

Application:

Psalm 56 shows us that it's okay to feel fear, but we don't have to let fear control us. We can bring our fears to God, trust in His protection, and find peace in His promises. Take time today to reflect on any fears or anxieties you may be facing. Bring them to God in prayer, trusting that He is for you and that He will provide comfort, deliverance, and peace. How can you practice living with a heart of gratitude, focusing on God's faithfulness, even in difficult times?

Prayer:

Lord, when I am afraid, I will trust in You. Thank You for being my refuge and my strength. You see my struggles and my fears, and I trust that You are always with me. Help me to focus on Your promises and to rest in Your peace. May I live with the confidence that You are for me and that You will never leave me. Thank You for being my deliverer and for filling my heart with gratitude. Amen.

Memorization Guide:
Step 1: Break Down the Psalm into Sections
1. **Verses 1-4**: A cry for mercy in times of fear and oppression.
2. **Verses 5-7**: Confidence in God's protection and the promise of justice.
3. **Verses 8-13**: Gratitude for God's deliverance and commitment to praise.

Step 2: Memorize by Key Themes and Visualizations
- **Section 1**: Crying out for mercy (visualize bringing your fears and anxieties to God).
- **Section 2**: Trusting in God's protection (visualize God's strong hand holding you in times of trouble).
- **Section 3**: Offering gratitude for deliverance (visualize yourself offering thanks and praise to God).

Verses:
- "When I am afraid, I put my trust in you."
- "You have kept count of my tossings; put my tears in your bottle."
- "This I know, that God is for me."

- "For you have delivered my soul from death, and my feet from falling."

Step 3: Repetition and Recitation
1. Memorize one section at a time.
2. Gradually combine the sections into the full psalm.
3. Recite the psalm daily, visualizing the key themes.

Summary of Key Images:
- Trusting God in times of fear.
- God's protection and deliverance.
- A heart of gratitude in response to God's faithfulness.

Psalm 61 – Seeking God's Protection and Comfort

"Hear my cry, O God; listen to my prayer. From the end of the earth I call to you, when my heart is faint. Lead me to the rock that is higher than I; for you have been my refuge, a strong tower against the enemy. Let me dwell in your tent forever; find refuge under the shelter of your wings. Selah. For you, O God, have heard my vows; you have given me the heritage of those who fear your name. Prolong the life of the king; may his years endure to all generations! May he be enthroned forever before God; appoint steadfast love and faithfulness to watch over him! So will I ever sing praises to your name, as I perform my vows day after day." – Psalm 61 (NRSV)

Reflection:
Psalm 61 is a heartfelt prayer for God's protection, guidance, and comfort during a time of distress. David, the psalmist, cries out to God from a place of weakness, asking for refuge and a solid foundation in times of trouble. In the midst of his feelings of being overwhelmed and fainthearted, he turns to God as his refuge, symbolized by the "rock that is higher than I." This psalm encourages us to seek God when we feel weak or uncertain, to trust in His strength, and to find shelter in His presence. It also reminds us of the power of praise and the importance of living in covenant with God.

Crying Out to God for Help
David begins the psalm by crying out to God, acknowledging that his heart is faint and in need of God's guidance and protection. When we face overwhelming situations, it's natural to feel faint-hearted, but David shows us the importance of calling on God, even in our weakest moments. Reflect on your

own moments of distress. How have you cried out to God in your own life? What does it look like for you to bring your burdens before God, trusting Him to hear and answer you?

Related Verses:
- **Psalm 34:17** – "When the righteous cry for help, the Lord hears and delivers them out of all their troubles."
- **2 Corinthians 12:9** – "But he said to me, 'My grace is sufficient for you, for my power is made perfect in weakness.' Therefore I will boast all the more gladly of my weaknesses, so that the power of Christ may rest upon me."

Finding Shelter in God's Presence

David's prayer moves to a plea for refuge under God's wings. This imagery of God's protection as a safe shelter is powerful, reminding us that God offers security in the midst of life's storms. David yearns to dwell in God's presence, and he recognizes that this is where true safety and peace are found. Reflect on how you experience God's presence as a place of refuge. How does spending time in God's presence help you find peace and security, especially when life feels chaotic?

Related Verses:
- **Psalm 91:4** – "He will cover you with his pinions, and under his wings you will find refuge; his faithfulness is a shield and buckler."
- **Matthew 23:37** – "O Jerusalem, Jerusalem, the city that kills the prophets and stones those who are sent to it! How often would I have gathered your children together as a hen gathers her brood under her wings, and you were not willing!"

The Rock that is Higher than I

David seeks the "rock that is higher than I," which symbolizes God as a firm, unshakable refuge. When we feel vulnerable or weak, God provides a rock, something higher and stronger than our own ability to cope. Reflect on how God has been a "rock" for you in times of weakness. When life feels shaky, where do you look for stability? How can you rely on God as your unshakable foundation?

Related Verses:
- **Psalm 18:2** – "The Lord is my rock and my fortress and my deliverer, my God, my rock, in whom I take refuge, my shield and the horn of my salvation, my stronghold."
- **Isaiah 26:4** – "Trust in the Lord forever, for the Lord God is an everlasting rock."

A Promise of Covenant and Protection

David acknowledges that God has heard his vows and has given him a heritage, the blessing of those who fear God. God is faithful to His covenant and offers His protection to those who belong to Him. David's confidence in God's care and love is evident in his prayer, as he asks God to prolong the king's life and establish His rule through steadfast love and faithfulness. Reflect on the promises of God's covenant and how His faithfulness to His people provides assurance in times of need. How does knowing that you are part of God's covenant family bring you peace and confidence?

Related Verses:
- **Psalm 103:17** – "But the steadfast love of the Lord is from everlasting to everlasting on those who fear him, and his righteousness to children's children."

- **2 Samuel 7:16** – "And your house and your kingdom shall be made sure forever before me. Your throne shall be established forever."

Praise and Gratitude for God's Deliverance

David resolves to praise God for His deliverance, promising to sing praises to God's name and fulfill his vows to Him. Worship is not only a response to God's blessings, but also an act of faith in God's character and promises. Reflect on how your response to God's faithfulness and protection can be an ongoing life of praise. How can you make praise a regular part of your relationship with God, acknowledging His presence, protection, and provision?

Related Verses:
- **Psalm 34:1** – "I will bless the Lord at all times; his praise shall continually be in my mouth."
- **Hebrews 13:15** – "Through him then let us continually offer up a sacrifice of praise to God, that is, the fruit of lips that acknowledge his name."

Quote:
"God's presence is a refuge, not only for the difficult moments but as the place we find our strength to move forward, day by day." – Charles Stanley

Application:

Psalm 61 calls us to seek God's refuge in times of distress, trust in His protection, and live with an ongoing attitude of praise. Reflect on the current season of your life and ask yourself: Where do I need to seek refuge in God? What areas of my life do I need to bring to God in prayer, trusting Him to be my rock and shelter? How can I respond to God's faithfulness with praise and gratitude?

Prayer:

Lord, I cry out to You for refuge and protection. When my heart is faint and my circumstances seem overwhelming, I trust in Your strength and Your loving presence. Thank You for being my rock and my shelter, a place of safety and peace. Help me to remain in Your presence and to offer You praise continually. I trust that You are faithful, and I will live in gratitude for Your deliverance. Amen.

Memorization Guide:

Step 1: Break Down the Psalm into Sections

1. **Verses 1-4**: A cry for help and a request for refuge.

2. **Verses 5-8**: Confidence in God's protection, promises, and faithfulness.

Step 2: Memorize by Key Themes and Visualizations

- **Section 1**: Seeking God as our refuge (visualize seeking shelter under God's wings).

- **Section 2**: Trusting in God's protection and promises (visualize standing on a solid rock that is higher than you).

Verses:

- "Lead me to the rock that is higher than I; for you have been my refuge, a strong tower against the enemy."

- "For you, O God, have heard my vows; you have given me the heritage of those who fear your name."

- "So will I ever sing praises to your name, as I perform my vows day after day."

Step 3: Repetition and Recitation

1. Memorize one section at a time.
2. Gradually combine the sections into the full psalm.
3. Recite the psalm daily, visualizing the key themes.

Summary of Key Images:

- Seeking God as our refuge and rock.
- Trusting in God's promises and protection.
- Praising God for His faithfulness and deliverance.

Psalm 62 – Trusting in God Alone

"For God alone my soul waits in silence; from him comes my salvation. He alone is my rock and my salvation, my fortress; I shall not be greatly shaken. How long will all of you attack a man to batter him, like a leaning wall, a tottering fence? They only plan to thrust him down from his high position. They take pleasure in falsehood. They bless with their mouths, but inwardly they curse. Selah. For God alone, O my soul, wait in silence, for my hope is from him. He only is my rock and my salvation, my fortress; I shall not be shaken. On God rests my salvation and my glory; my mighty rock, my refuge is God. Trust in him at all times, O people; pour out your heart before him; God is a refuge for us. Selah. Those of low estate are but a breath; those of high estate are a delusion; in the balances they go up; they are together lighter than a breath. Put no trust in extortion; set no vain hopes on robbery; if riches increase, set not your heart on them. Once God has spoken; twice have I heard this: that power belongs to God, and that to you, O Lord, belongs steadfast love. For you will render to a man according to his work." – Psalm 62 (NRSV)

Reflection:

Psalm 62 is a powerful declaration of trust in God as the only source of security, salvation, and refuge. In the face of adversity, David confidently places his hope in God alone, resisting the temptations to trust in wealth, power, or human praise. The psalm invites us to examine where we place our trust and reminds us that true peace comes from knowing that God is our rock and refuge. Whether we are facing personal struggles or the pressures of society, we can find rest in God's steadfast love and power. This psalm calls us to place our hope in God alone, who is worthy of our trust and reliance.

Waiting in Silence for God Alone

David begins the psalm with a declaration that his soul waits in silence for God alone. Silence in this context represents a soul that is at peace, waiting on God without anxiety or rushing to make things happen. It's a posture of trust and surrender. Reflect on the areas of your life where you may need to practice waiting in silence before God, trusting that He will bring about His will in His perfect time. How does silence before God help you hear His voice more clearly and trust in His timing?

Related Verses:

- **Psalm 37:7** – "Be still before the Lord and wait patiently for him; fret not yourself over the one who prospers in his way, over the man who carries out evil devices."
- **Isaiah 40:31** – "But they who wait for the Lord shall renew their strength; they shall mount up with wings like eagles; they shall run and not be weary; they shall walk and not faint."

God as Our Rock and Salvation

David repeats several times that God alone is his rock, salvation, and fortress. These images of God as a rock and fortress symbolize His stability, protection, and strength in times of danger or difficulty. Reflect on how you experience God as your rock and salvation. When life feels unstable or when you face challenges, how can you lean on God as your unshakable foundation? How can you cultivate a deeper trust in God's ability to protect and deliver you?

Related Verses:

- **Psalm 18:2** – "The Lord is my rock and my fortress and my deliverer, my God, my rock, in whom I take refuge, my shield and the horn of my salvation, my stronghold."

- **2 Samuel 22:47** – "The Lord lives, and blessed be my rock, and exalted be my God, the rock of my salvation."

The Futility of Trusting in Human Power

David warns against trusting in human power, wealth, or status. He describes how people of high and low estate are both ultimately fragile and temporary. Even those who are rich or in positions of power are not dependable in the way that God is. Reflect on your own tendencies to place trust in things other than God—whether it's wealth, status, human approval, or your own strength. How can you shift your focus back to God as the only true source of security, even in a world that often celebrates material success and worldly power?

Related Verses:

- **Proverbs 23:4-5** – "Do not toil to acquire wealth; be discerning enough to desist. When your eyes light on it, it is gone, for suddenly it sprouts wings, flying like an eagle toward heaven."

- **Jeremiah 9:23-24** – "Thus says the Lord: Let not the wise man boast in his wisdom, let not the mighty man boast in his might, let not the rich man boast in his riches, but let him who boasts boast in this, that he understands and knows me, that I am the Lord who practices steadfast love, justice, and righteousness in the earth."

Trusting God at All Times

David calls the people to trust in God at all times, pouring out their hearts before Him. This act of pouring out one's heart is a picture of complete vulnerability and dependence on God. Reflect on your relationship with God. How often do you pour out your heart to Him, sharing your struggles, desires, and fears?

How can you deepen your trust in God by bringing all of yourself—your emotions, questions, and concerns—before Him, knowing that He is a refuge for us?

Related Verses:
- **1 Peter 5:7** – "Casting all your anxieties on him, because he cares for you."
- **Psalm 62:8** – "Trust in him at all times, O people; pour out your heart before him; God is a refuge for us."

God's Power and Steadfast Love

David acknowledges that all power belongs to God and that God's steadfast love is essential to His character. God's love is not fickle or conditional, but unwavering and consistent. Reflect on the ways God has demonstrated His power and love in your life. How does knowing that God is all-powerful and always loving give you confidence in your daily life? How can you trust in His love more deeply as you face challenges?

Related Verses:
- **Romans 8:38-39** – "For I am sure that neither death nor life, nor angels nor rulers, nor things present nor things to come, nor powers, nor height nor depth, nor anything else in all creation, will be able to separate us from the love of God in Christ Jesus our Lord."
- **Psalm 136:1** – "Give thanks to the Lord, for he is good, for his steadfast love endures forever."

Quote:
"When we rely on God, we find that He is our security, our strength, and our eternal foundation." – Charles Stanley

---

Application:
Psalm 62 calls us to place our trust in God alone, recognizing

that He is our rock, our refuge, and our salvation. Take time today to reflect on where you have placed your trust. Is there anything in your life that you have relied on more than God? How can you shift your focus back to trusting God as your ultimate source of security? Whether you are in a season of calm or facing struggles, rest in the assurance that God is your unshakable foundation.

Prayer:
Lord, You are my rock, my fortress, and my salvation. In times of uncertainty, I trust in Your steadfast love and Your power to protect and guide me. Help me to rely on You and not on the fleeting things of this world. I choose to pour out my heart before You and to trust in Your perfect timing and plans. Thank You for being my refuge, my strength, and my security. Amen.

Memorization Guide:
Step 1: Break Down the Psalm into Sections
1. **Verses 1-4**: A declaration of trust in God and a description of enemies.
2. **Verses 5-7**: Reaffirming trust in God as the source of salvation and refuge.
3. **Verses 8-12**: A call to trust in God and not in wealth or power, acknowledging God's power and love.

Step 2: Memorize by Key Themes and Visualizations
- **Section 1**: Trusting in God alone (visualize God as your rock and refuge).
- **Section 2**: Acknowledging the futility of trusting in human power (visualize earthly treasures fading away).

- **Section 3**: Trusting in God's love and power (visualize God's love as an unshakable foundation).

Verses:
- "For God alone my soul waits in silence; from him comes my salvation."
- "Trust in him at all times, O people; pour out your heart before him; God is a refuge for us."
- "Once God has spoken; twice have I heard this: that power belongs to God, and that to you, O Lord, belongs steadfast love."

Step 3: Repetition and Recitation
1. Memorize one section at a time.
2. Gradually combine the sections into the full psalm.
3. Recite the psalm daily, visualizing the key themes.

Summary of Key Images:
- God as our rock and refuge.
- The futility of trusting in wealth and power.
- Resting in God's steadfast love and power.

Psalm 65: Praising God for His Abundant Provision
Psalm 65 (NRSV):

Praise is due to you, O God, in Zion; and to you shall vows be performed, O you who answer prayer! To you all flesh shall come. When deeds of iniquity overwhelm us, you forgive our transgressions. Happy are those whom you choose and bring near to live in your courts. We shall be satisfied with the goodness of your house, your holy temple.

By awesome deeds you answer us with deliverance, O God of our salvation; you are the hope of all the ends of the earth and of the farthest seas. By your strength you established the mountains; you are girded with might. You silence the roaring of the seas, the roaring of their waves, the tumult of the peoples. Those who live at earth's farthest bounds are awed by your signs; you make the gateways of the morning and the evening shout for joy.

You visit the earth and water it, you greatly enrich it; the river of God is full of water; you provide the people with grain, for so you have prepared it. You water its furrows abundantly, settling its ridges, softening it with showers, and blessing its growth. You crown the year with your bounty; your wagon tracks overflow with richness. The pastures of the wilderness overflow, the hills gird themselves with joy, the meadows clothe themselves with flocks, the valleys deck themselves with grain, they shout and sing together for joy.

Reflection:

Psalm 65 is a celebration of God's abundant provision and His care for all creation. The psalmist opens with praise for God, who forgives sins and invites His people into His presence. This psalm reminds us of God's generosity in sustaining both the earth and His people, and it paints a vivid picture of nature responding joyfully to God's care.

Gratefulness for Forgiveness and Nearness to God
The psalmist begins with gratitude for God's mercy, emphasizing that those who are invited into God's presence are truly blessed. Reflect on the joy and peace that come from being forgiven and having access to God's presence. This closeness with God is a treasure that surpasses all else.
Related Verse: Psalm 84:4 – "Happy are those who live in your house, ever singing your praise."

God's Power Over Creation
Psalm 65 celebrates God's sovereignty over the natural world. His power is evident in the mountains, seas, and skies, all of which respond to His mighty acts. This portion of the psalm reminds us that God's majesty is seen in every part of creation, from towering mountains to quiet streams. Take a moment to appreciate the beauty around you as a testament to God's greatness.
Related Verse: Jeremiah 10:12 – "It is he who made the earth by his power, who established the world by his wisdom, and by his understanding stretched out the heavens."

God's Abundant Provision
In the final verses, the psalmist describes how God blesses the earth, providing rain, grain, and fruitful harvests. The imagery of overflowing fields, green hills, and bountiful valleys speaks to God's faithful provision. Just as God cares for the earth, He provides for us, often beyond what we expect or imagine.
Related Verse: Philippians 4:19 – "And my God will fully satisfy every need of yours according to his riches in glory in Christ Jesus."

After HIS Own Heart

Quote:
"God is more ready to give than we are to ask." – St. Augustine

Application:
This week, practice gratitude for God's abundant provision in your life. Whether it's food, shelter, relationships, or spiritual blessings, take time to acknowledge and thank God for His generosity. Notice the ways He has provided for you and commit to sharing that blessing with others as you're able. Let your gratitude be a reflection of trust in His continued faithfulness.

Prayer:
Lord, thank You for the countless ways You provide for me. You are the Creator of all things, and You sustain the earth and my life with Your abundant care. Help me to live with a grateful heart, trusting in Your provision, and delighting in the joy of Your presence. Amen.

Memorization Guide:
Step 1: Break Down Key Sections
1. Verses 1-4: Gratefulness for God's forgiveness and nearness.
2. Verses 5-8: Celebrating God's power over creation.
3. Verses 9-13: God's abundant provision for the earth.

Step 2: Memorize by Key Themes and Visualizations
Section 1: Gratitude for God's Forgiveness (Verses 1-4)
- Visualize the joy of entering God's presence with a thankful heart.

Section 2: God's Power in Creation (Verses 5-8)
- Imagine mountains, seas, and skies, all displaying God's majesty.

Section 3: God's Provision for the Earth (Verses 9-13)
- Picture fields overflowing with grain, green hills, and valleys full of life.

Summary of Key Images
- Entering God's presence with gratitude and forgiveness.
- God's power displayed in mountains, seas, and skies.
- Fields and valleys overflowing, reflecting God's faithful provision.

Psalm 66: Shout for Joy to God, All the Earth
Psalm 66 (NRSV):

Make a joyful noise to God, all the earth; sing the glory of his name; give to him glorious praise. Say to God, "How awesome are your deeds! Because of your great power, your enemies cringe before you. All the earth worships you; they sing praises to you, sing praises to your name."

Come and see what God has done: he is awesome in his deeds among mortals. He turned the sea into dry land; they passed through the river on foot. There we rejoiced in him, who rules by his might forever, whose eyes keep watch on the nations—let the rebellious not exalt themselves. Bless our God, O peoples, let the sound of his praise be heard, who has kept us among the living, and has not let our feet slip.

For you, O God, have tested us; you have tried us as silver is tried. You brought us into the net; you laid burdens on our backs; you let people ride over our heads; we went through fire and through water; yet you have brought us out to a spacious place. I will come into your house with burnt offerings; I will pay you my vows, those that my lips uttered and my mouth promised when I was in trouble. I will offer to you burnt offerings of fatlings, with the smoke of the sacrifice of rams; I will make an offering of bulls and goats.

Come and hear, all you who fear God, and I will tell what he has done for me. I cried aloud to him, and he was extolled with my tongue. If I had cherished iniquity in my heart, the Lord would not have listened. But truly God has listened; he has given heed to the words of my prayer. Blessed be God, because he has not rejected my prayer or removed his steadfast love from me.

Reflection:
Psalm 66 is a joyful declaration of God's mighty works and a

celebration of His faithfulness in answering prayer. This psalm calls on all creation to praise God and recognize His power, justice, and mercy. From recounting Israel's deliverance to personal testimony, Psalm 66 reminds us that God is actively involved in our lives, shaping us through trials and sustaining us with His love.

God's Mighty Works in Creation

The psalmist opens by inviting "all the earth" to make a joyful noise to God. This universal call to worship highlights that God's deeds are worthy of global praise. Reflect on how creation itself—oceans, mountains, forests—testify to God's greatness and how our praise should echo that magnificence.

Related Verse: Psalm 19:1 – "The heavens declare the glory of God; the skies proclaim the work of his hands."

God's Deliverance and Faithfulness

Verses 5-12 recount God's past faithfulness, specifically His deliverance of Israel at the Red Sea. The psalmist also speaks of trials and testing, likening them to the refining process of silver. God uses challenges to strengthen our faith and lead us into a "spacious place." Consider how past struggles have prepared you for greater growth and reliance on God.

Related Verse: James 1:2-4 – "Consider it pure joy, my brothers and sisters, whenever you face trials of many kinds, because you know that the testing of your faith produces perseverance."

Gratitude for Answered Prayer

The psalm concludes with a personal testimony of answered prayer, demonstrating that God listens to those who seek Him earnestly. This portion of the psalm encourages us to reflect on specific instances when God has heard and responded to our prayers, deepening our gratitude and trust in Him.

Related Verse: 1 John 5:14 – "This is the confidence we have in approaching God: that if we ask anything according to his will, he hears us."

Quote:
"God shapes the world by prayer. The more prayer there is in the world, the better the world will be." – E.M. Bounds

Application:
This week, set aside intentional time to reflect on God's faithfulness in your life. Consider the ways He has answered prayers and guided you through difficulties. Write these experiences down as a personal testimony, and share them with someone as an encouragement of God's steadfast love and care. Let this be a reminder to continue seeking Him in every situation.

Prayer:
Lord, I praise You for Your mighty works and the way You listen to my prayers. Thank You for shaping my life through both blessings and trials, leading me into a place of greater trust in You. Help me to share Your faithfulness with others, that they may be encouraged to seek You as well. Amen.

Memorization Guide:
Step 1: Break Down Key Sections
1. Verses 1-4: A call for all creation to praise God.
2. Verses 5-12: Recounting God's deliverance and refining.
3. Verses 13-20: Grateful testimony for answered prayer.

Step 2: Memorize by Key Themes and Visualizations

Section 1: Universal Praise (Verses 1-4)
- Picture all creation singing joyfully to God.

Section 2: God's Deliverance (Verses 5-12)
- Visualize Israel's deliverance at the Red Sea and the refining process.

Section 3: Testimony of Prayer (Verses 13-20)
- Recall personal experiences of answered prayer as a source of gratitude.

Summary of Key Images
- All creation joyfully praising God.
- God refining us through trials like silver.
- Personal testimony of answered prayer as a reminder of God's faithfulness.

Psalm 66: Shout for Joy to God, All the Earth
Psalm 66 (NRSV):

Make a joyful noise to God, all the earth; sing the glory of his name; give to him glorious praise. Say to God, "How awesome are your deeds! Because of your great power, your enemies cringe before you. All the earth worships you; they sing praises to you, sing praises to your name."

Come and see what God has done: he is awesome in his deeds among mortals. He turned the sea into dry land; they passed through the river on foot. There we rejoiced in him, who rules by his might forever, whose eyes keep watch on the nations—let the rebellious not exalt themselves. Bless our God, O peoples, let the sound of his praise be heard, who has kept us among the living, and has not let our feet slip.

For you, O God, have tested us; you have tried us as silver is tried. You brought us into the net; you laid burdens on our backs; you let people ride over our heads; we went through fire and through water; yet you have brought us out to a spacious place. I will come into your house with burnt offerings; I will pay you my vows, those that my lips uttered and my mouth promised when I was in trouble. I will offer to you burnt offerings of fatlings, with the smoke of the sacrifice of rams; I will make an offering of bulls and goats.

Come and hear, all you who fear God, and I will tell what he has done for me. I cried aloud to him, and he was extolled with my tongue. If I had cherished iniquity in my heart, the Lord would not have listened. But truly God has listened; he has given heed to the words of my prayer. Blessed be God, because he has not rejected my prayer or removed his steadfast love from me.

Reflection:

Psalm 66 is a joyful declaration of God's mighty works and

a celebration of His faithfulness in answering prayer. This psalm calls on all creation to praise God and recognize His power, justice, and mercy. From recounting Israel's deliverance to personal testimony, Psalm 66 reminds us that God is actively involved in our lives, shaping us through trials and sustaining us with His love.

God's Mighty Works in Creation

The psalmist opens by inviting "all the earth" to make a joyful noise to God. This universal call to worship highlights that God's deeds are worthy of global praise. Reflect on how creation itself—oceans, mountains, forests—testify to God's greatness and how our praise should echo that magnificence.

Related Verse: Psalm 19:1 – "The heavens declare the glory of God; the skies proclaim the work of his hands."

God's Deliverance and Faithfulness

Verses 5-12 recount God's past faithfulness, specifically His deliverance of Israel at the Red Sea. The psalmist also speaks of trials and testing, likening them to the refining process of silver. God uses challenges to strengthen our faith and lead us into a "spacious place." Consider how past struggles have prepared you for greater growth and reliance on God.

Related Verse: James 1:2-4 – "Consider it pure joy, my brothers and sisters, whenever you face trials of many kinds, because you know that the testing of your faith produces perseverance."

Gratitude for Answered Prayer

The psalm concludes with a personal testimony of

answered prayer, demonstrating that God listens to those who seek Him earnestly. This portion of the psalm encourages us to reflect on specific instances when God has heard and responded to our prayers, deepening our gratitude and trust in Him.

Related Verse: 1 John 5:14 – "This is the confidence we have in approaching God: that if we ask anything according to his will, he hears us."

Quote:

"God shapes the world by prayer. The more prayer there is in the world, the better the world will be." – E.M. Bounds

Application:

This week, set aside intentional time to reflect on God's faithfulness in your life. Consider the ways He has answered prayers and guided you through difficulties. Write these experiences down as a personal testimony, and share them with someone as an encouragement of God's steadfast love and care. Let this be a reminder to continue seeking Him in every situation.

Prayer:

Lord, I praise You for Your mighty works and the way You listen to my prayers. Thank You for shaping my life through both blessings and trials, leading me into a place of greater trust in You. Help me to share Your faithfulness with others, that they may be encouraged to seek You as well. Amen.

Memorization Guide:
Step 1: Break Down Key Sections

1. Verses 1-4: A call for all creation to praise God.
2. Verses 5-12: Recounting God's deliverance and refining.
3. Verses 13-20: Grateful testimony for answered prayer.

Step 2: Memorize by Key Themes and Visualizations

Section 1: Universal Praise (Verses 1-4)
- Picture all creation singing joyfully to God.

Section 2: God's Deliverance (Verses 5-12)
- Visualize Israel's deliverance at the Red Sea and the refining process.

Section 3: Testimony of Prayer (Verses 13-20)
- Recall personal experiences of answered prayer as a source of gratitude.

Summary of Key Images
- All creation joyfully praising God.
- God refining us through trials like silver.
- Personal testimony of answered prayer as a reminder of God's faithfulness.

Psalm 67: A Prayer for Blessing and Praise to All Nations
Psalm 67 (NRSV):

May God be gracious to us and bless us and make his face to shine upon us, that your way may be known upon earth, your saving power among all nations. Let the peoples praise you, O God; let all the peoples praise you. Let the nations be glad and sing for joy, for you judge the peoples with equity and guide the nations upon earth. Let the peoples praise you, O God; let all the peoples praise you.

The earth has yielded its increase; God, our God, has blessed us. May God continue to bless us; let all the ends of the earth revere him.

Reflection:

Psalm 67 is a beautiful and concise prayer for God's blessing on His people, not only for their own sake but so that all nations may come to know His goodness and salvation. The psalmist envisions a world where God's people shine His light, leading all nations to rejoice in God's justice, mercy, and provision.

Blessed to Be a Blessing

The psalm begins with a prayer for blessing that recalls the priestly blessing in Numbers 6:24-26. This blessing asks for God's favor and presence, not just for the individual's sake, but so that God's ways and salvation might be known throughout the world. Reflect on how your life can be a channel of God's blessing to others, helping them to see His love and mercy.

Related Verse: Numbers 6:24-26 – "The Lord bless you and keep you; the Lord make his face to shine upon you, and be gracious to you; the Lord lift up his countenance upon you, and give you peace."

God's Justice and Guidance for All Nations

In verses 3-4, the psalmist prays that all people will praise God and rejoice because of His just and righteous rule. God's justice is a reason for joy, as He rules with equity and fairness. This part of the psalm reminds us to pray for God's guidance over all nations and for people of every culture to experience the joy and peace that come from His rule.

Related Verse: Isaiah 2:4 – "He shall judge between the nations, and shall arbitrate for many peoples; they shall beat their swords into plowshares, and their spears into pruning hooks; nation shall not lift up sword against nation, neither shall they learn war anymore."

Praise for God's Provision
The closing verses celebrate God's provision as the earth yields its harvest, a symbol of His faithful care. The psalmist asks for continued blessings so that all people, to the very ends of the earth, will come to revere and worship God. Consider how God's provision in your life can be a testament to others of His goodness.

Related Verse: Psalm 85:12 – "The Lord will indeed give what is good, and our land will yield its harvest."

Quote:
"God blesses us to be a blessing to others, spreading His love and kindness across the earth." – Billy Graham

Application:
This week, think of practical ways to extend God's blessing to those around you. Whether through an encouraging word, a small act of kindness, or a prayer for others, seek to reflect God's goodness. Consider how your actions might help others see

After HIS Own Heart

God's love and draw closer to Him. Let your life be a light that points to His salvation.

Prayer:

Lord, thank You for Your abundant blessings. May Your face shine upon me, and may my life reflect Your love and kindness. Help me to share Your blessings with others so that all people might know Your saving grace and worship You. Guide the nations with Your justice, and let all the earth sing of Your goodness. Amen.

Memorization Guide:

Step 1: Break Down Key Sections

1. Verses 1-2: A prayer for God's blessing to be known among the nations.

2. Verses 3-4: Praise for God's just rule over all people.

3. Verses 5-7: Celebration of God's provision and a call for all to revere Him.

Step 2: Memorize by Key Themes and Visualizations

Section 1: Blessing for God's Glory (Verses 1-2)
- Picture God's light shining on His people, spreading His ways.

Section 2: Joy in God's Justice (Verses 3-4)
- Imagine nations singing with joy at God's righteous rule.

Section 3: Praise for God's Provision (Verses 5-7)
- Visualize a bountiful harvest and the world revering God.

Summary of Key Images
- God's face shining upon His people, blessing them.

- Nations rejoicing and praising God for His justice.
- The earth yielding a bountiful harvest as a symbol of God's provision.

Psalm 69: Crying Out in Distress and Finding God's Salvation
Psalm 69 (NRSV):

Save me, O God, for the waters have come up to my neck. I sink in deep mire, where there is no foothold; I have come into deep waters, and the flood sweeps over me. I am weary with my crying; my throat is parched. My eyes grow dim with waiting for my God. More in number than the hairs of my head are those who hate me without cause; many are those who would destroy me, my enemies who accuse me falsely. What I did not steal must I now restore? O God, you know my folly; the wrongs I have done are not hidden from you. Do not let those who hope in you be put to shame because of me, O Lord God of hosts; do not let those who seek you be dishonored because of me, O God of Israel. It is for your sake that I have borne reproach, that shame has covered my face. I have become a stranger to my kindred, an alien to my mother's children. It is zeal for your house that has consumed me; the insults of those who insult you have fallen on me. When I humbled my soul with fasting, they insulted me for doing so. When I made sackcloth my clothing, I became a byword to them. I am the subject of gossip for those who sit in the gate, and the drunkards make songs about me.

But as for me, my prayer is to you, O Lord. At an acceptable time, O God, in the abundance of your steadfast love, answer me. With your faithful help, rescue me from sinking in the mire; let me be delivered from my enemies and from the deep waters. Do not let the flood sweep over me, or the deep swallow me up, or the Pit close its mouth over me. Answer me, O Lord, for your steadfast love is good; according to your abundant mercy, turn to me. Do not hide your face from your servant, for I am in distress—make haste to answer me. Draw near to me, redeem me, set me free because of my enemies.

You know the insults I receive, and my shame and dishonor; my foes are all known to you. Insults have broken my heart, so that I am in despair. I looked for pity, but there was none; and for comforters, but I found none. They gave me poison for food, and for my thirst they gave me vinegar to drink. Let their table be a trap for them, a snare for their allies. Let their eyes be darkened so that they cannot see, and make their loins tremble continually. Pour out your indignation upon them, and let your burning anger overtake them. May their camp be a desolation; let no one live in their tents. For they persecute those whom you have struck down, and those whom you have wounded, they attack still more. Add guilt to their guilt; may they have no acquittal from you. Let them be blotted out of the book of the living; let them not be enrolled among the righteous.

But I am lowly and in pain; let your salvation, O God, protect me. I will praise the name of God with a song; I will magnify him with thanksgiving. This will please the Lord more than an ox or a bull with horns and hoofs. Let the oppressed see it and be glad; you who seek God, let your hearts revive. For the Lord hears the needy, and does not despise his own that are in bonds. Let heaven and earth praise him, the seas and everything that moves in them. For God will save Zion and rebuild the cities of Judah; and his servants shall live there and possess it; the children of his servants shall inherit it, and those who love his name shall live in it.

Reflection:
Psalm 69 is a powerful expression of distress and anguish, yet it reveals a deep trust in God amidst overwhelming trials. David cries out to God, overwhelmed by his troubles, and feels as though he is sinking in a relentless flood. This psalm captures the raw human experience of feeling abandoned and powerless,

yet it also points us toward hope and salvation in God.

Holding on in Deep Waters
The opening verses highlight a feeling of drowning in sorrow and affliction. David's plea is not only for help but also for understanding. These verses remind us that even in our darkest hours, God hears us and sees us. Reflect on the places in your life where you feel like the waters are rising, and take comfort in knowing that God is there, ready to lift you up.
Related Verse: Isaiah 43:2 – "When you pass through the waters, I will be with you; and through the rivers, they shall not overwhelm you."

Faithfulness Despite False Accusations
Psalm 69:7-12 describes how David faces ridicule and false accusations. He endures shame for God's sake, a theme that foreshadows the suffering of Christ. This part of the psalm is a reminder that being faithful may sometimes bring rejection or misunderstanding from others, but God's approval is our ultimate reward.
Related Verse: Matthew 5:10-11 – "Blessed are those who are persecuted for righteousness' sake, for theirs is the kingdom of heaven. Blessed are you when people revile you and persecute you and utter all kinds of evil against you falsely on my account."

Trust in God's Redemption
Amidst his suffering, David's hope in God remains unshaken. In verse 13, he shifts from lament to faith, praying, "But as for me, my prayer is to you, O LORD. At an acceptable time, O God, in the abundance of your steadfast love, answer me." This verse reflects the confidence that God's timing and love are perfect, even when we do not yet see the answer.
Related Verse: Romans 5:3-4 – "And not only that, but we also

boast in our sufferings, knowing that suffering produces endurance, and endurance produces character, and character produces hope."

Quote:
"God is our refuge and strength, a very present help in trouble. Therefore we will not fear, though the earth should change, though the mountains shake in the heart of the sea." – Corrie Ten Boom

Application:
Reflect on any areas where you feel burdened or overwhelmed. Are there accusations or challenges you face for standing firm in faith? Bring these before God in prayer, trusting in His salvation and timing. Take comfort in knowing that, like David, you can cry out to God who listens and responds with love and redemption.

Prayer:
Lord, in my distress, I turn to You. Save me from the depths that threaten to overwhelm me. Grant me patience and strength to endure hardship for Your sake, knowing that You are with me in every trial. Help me to trust in Your timing and Your steadfast love. Amen.

Memorization Guide:
Step 1: Break Down Key Sections
1. **Verses 1-3:** David's plea for rescue from overwhelming distress.
2. **Verses 7-12:** Faithfulness in the face of mockery and false accusations.

3. **Verse 13:** Turning to God with hope and trust in His steadfast love.

Step 2: Memorize by Key Themes and Visualizations
Section 1: David's Plea (Verses 1-3)
- Visualize David reaching out in distress, confident in God's rescue.

Section 2: Faithfulness Amidst Ridicule (Verses 7-12)
- Picture David remaining steadfast despite insults.

Section 3: Trust in God's Love (Verse 13)
- Imagine David's transition from despair to confident hope.

Summary of Key Images
- Overwhelmed by water but calling out in faith.
- Enduring mockery for God's sake.
- Trusting in God's response and timing.

Psalm 73: Finding God as Our Ultimate Strength and Portion
Psalm 73 (NRSV):

Truly God is good to the upright, to those who are pure in heart. But as for me, my feet had almost stumbled; my steps had nearly slipped. For I was envious of the arrogant; I saw the prosperity of the wicked. For they have no pain; their bodies are sound and sleek. They are not in trouble as others are; they are not plagued like other people. Therefore pride is their necklace; violence covers them like a garment. Their eyes swell out with fatness; their hearts overflow with follies. They scoff and speak with malice; loftily they threaten oppression. They set their mouths against heaven, and their tongues range over the earth. Therefore the people turn and praise them, and find no fault in them. And they say, "How can God know? Is there knowledge in the Most High?" Such are the wicked; always at ease, they increase in riches. All in vain I have kept my heart clean and washed my hands in innocence. For all day long I have been plagued, and am punished every morning.

If I had said, "I will talk on in this way," I would have been untrue to the circle of your children. But when I thought how to understand this, it seemed to me a wearisome task, until I went into the sanctuary of God; then I perceived their end. Truly you set them in slippery places; you make them fall to ruin. How they are destroyed in a moment, swept away utterly by terrors! They are like a dream when one awakes; on awaking you despise their phantoms.

When my soul was embittered, when I was pricked in heart, I was stupid and ignorant; I was like a brute beast toward you. Nevertheless I am continually with you; you hold my right hand. You guide me with your counsel, and afterward you will receive me with honor. Whom have I in heaven but you? And there is nothing on earth that I desire other than you. My flesh and my heart may fail, but God is the strength of my heart and my portion forever. Indeed, those who are far from you will perish; you put an end to those who are false to you. But for me it is good to be near God; I have made the Lord God my refuge, to tell of all your works.

Reflection:
Psalm 73 takes us on a journey from envy and doubt to peace and assurance. The psalmist, Asaph, begins by expressing frustration over the prosperity of the wicked, feeling disheartened by their ease while he suffers. Yet, as he enters God's sanctuary, he gains a divine perspective, recognizing the ultimate end of those who are far from God. He concludes that God is his true strength and portion, the only One he needs.

Struggling with Envy and Doubt
The psalmist admits his envy of the wicked, observing their seemingly carefree lives. He feels that his efforts to stay pure are in vain. This part of the psalm is a reminder of our human tendency to compare ourselves to others and feel disheartened. It is only by turning to God that we find lasting perspective and peace.

Related Verse: Proverbs 23:17-18 – "Do not let your heart envy sinners, but always be zealous for the fear of the LORD. There is surely a future hope for you, and your hope will not be cut off."

A New Perspective in God's Presence
Entering the sanctuary brings clarity. The psalmist realizes that worldly prosperity is temporary and that ultimate security lies in God. When we focus on eternal truths rather than temporary successes, we gain peace and renewed strength. Reflect on how God's presence can shift your focus from earthly concerns

to eternal promises.

Related Verse: Matthew 6:19-21 – "Do not store up for yourselves treasures on earth, where moth and rust consume and where thieves break in and steal; but store up for yourselves treasures in heaven, where neither moth nor rust consumes and where thieves do not break in and steal. For where your treasure is, there your heart will be also."

God as Our Strength and Portion

The psalmist's closing declaration is a powerful statement of trust and satisfaction in God. Even if his health fails, he knows that God is his portion forever. This verse reminds us that God is our ultimate source of strength and contentment, far beyond any earthly gain.

Related Verse: Philippians 4:13 – "I can do all things through him who strengthens me."

Quote:

"When I cannot understand my Father's leading, I can trust His heart." – Charles Spurgeon

Application:

Reflect this week on areas in your life where envy, comparison, or doubt may have crept in. Bring these feelings before God, asking Him to renew your perspective. Focus on the eternal promises and blessings you have in Him, trusting that He is enough. Let your heart rest in the assurance that God is your strength and portion.

Prayer:

Lord, help me to see beyond the temporary and to rest in Your eternal promises. Renew my focus and remove any envy or doubt from my heart. You are my strength, my refuge, and my portion forever. Draw me close to You, and may I find true contentment in Your presence alone. Amen.

Memorization Guide:
Step 1: Break Down Key Sections

1. **Verses 1-14:** Struggling with envy and questioning the prosperity of the wicked.
2. **Verses 15-20:** Gaining clarity in God's presence and understanding the end of the wicked.
3. **Verses 21-28:** Finding strength and satisfaction in God as his portion.

Step 2: Memorize by Key Themes and Visualizations
Section 1: Struggle with Envy (Verses 1-14)

- Visualize the psalmist observing the wicked, then feeling frustrated.

Section 2: Divine Perspective (Verses 15-20)

- Imagine entering a peaceful sanctuary, gaining a new perspective on life.

Section 3: God as Our Portion (Verses 21-28)

- Picture finding strength in God alone, even as earthly things fade.

Summary of Key Images

- The psalmist's struggle with envy and frustration.
- Entering God's sanctuary for clarity and peace.
- Declaring God as his strength and eternal portion.

Psalm 77: Remembering God's Faithfulness in Times of Trouble
Psalm 77 (NRSV):

I cry aloud to God, aloud to God, that he may hear me. In the day of my trouble I seek the Lord; in the night my hand is stretched out without wearying; my soul refuses to be comforted. I think of God, and I moan; I meditate, and my spirit faints. You keep my eyelids from closing; I am so troubled that I cannot speak. I consider the days of old, and remember the years of long ago. I commune with my heart in the night; I meditate and search my spirit: "Will the Lord spurn forever, and never again be favorable? Has his steadfast love ceased forever? Are his promises at an end for all time? Has God forgotten to be gracious? Has he in anger shut up his compassion?" And I say, "It is my grief that the right hand of the Most High has changed."

I will call to mind the deeds of the Lord; I will remember your wonders of old. I will meditate on all your work, and muse on your mighty deeds. Your way, O God, is holy. What god is so great as our God? You are the God who works wonders; you have displayed your might among the peoples. With your strong arm you redeemed your people, the descendants of Jacob and Joseph. When the waters saw you, O God, when the waters saw you, they were afraid; the very deep trembled. The clouds poured out water; the skies thundered; your arrows flashed on every side. The crash of your thunder was in the whirlwind; your lightnings lit up the world; the earth trembled and shook. Your way was through the sea, your path, through the mighty waters; yet your footprints were unseen. You led your people like a flock by the hand of Moses and Aaron.

Reflection:

Psalm 77 reflects the journey from despair to hope as the

psalmist, Asaph, wrestles with deep anguish and seeks God in the silence. Initially, he feels unheard and abandoned, but as he recalls God's past faithfulness, his perspective shifts. This psalm teaches us that while pain and questioning are natural, remembering God's past mercies can renew our hope.

Seeking God in the Dark Night

The psalm opens with a heart burdened with trouble, reaching out to God even when comfort feels distant. This part of the psalm reminds us of the power of persistence in prayer. Even when we feel God is silent, we are invited to keep seeking Him with an honest heart.

Related Verse: Lamentations 3:25-26 – "The Lord is good to those who wait for him, to the soul that seeks him. It is good that one should wait quietly for the salvation of the Lord."

Recalling God's Mighty Deeds

Asaph turns his heart to remember God's works in verses 10-15. This shift reveals the importance of gratitude and reflection. By focusing on God's past miracles, Asaph finds strength and hope for the present. Reflect on moments when God's faithfulness was clear in your life, and allow those memories to reassure you in difficult times.

Related Verse: Isaiah 46:9 – "Remember the former things of old; for I am God, and there is no other; I am God, and there is none like me."

God's Unseen Path Through the Waters

Verses 16-20 conclude with a vivid recollection of God parting the Red Sea. Even when the path was unclear, God led His people to safety. This part of the psalm reminds us that God often works in ways we cannot see, guiding us through challenges toward a place of deliverance.

Related Verse: Exodus 14:21-22 – "Then Moses stretched out his hand over the sea; and the Lord drove the sea back by a strong east wind all night, and made the sea dry land, and the waters were divided."

Quote:
"Faith is taking the first step even when you don't see the whole staircase." – Martin Luther King Jr.

Application:
Take time this week to recall specific moments when God was faithful to you. Write them down or share them with a friend to solidify these memories in your heart. Use these reflections as fuel to trust God, even when He seems silent. Remember, God's track record of faithfulness is an anchor in every storm.

Prayer:
Lord, in my moments of distress, help me remember Your faithfulness. Remind me of the times You have brought me through trials and renewed my strength. Strengthen my heart to trust in You, even when I cannot see the way forward. Let my faith be rooted in Your past mercies and Your eternal love. Amen.

Memorization Guide:
Step 1: Break Down Key Sections
1. Verses 1-4: Crying out to God in despair.
2. Verses 10-15: Remembering God's mighty deeds.
3. Verses 16-20: Trusting in God's unseen path through the waters.

Step 2: Memorize by Key Themes and Visualizations

Section 1: Crying Out in Despair (Verses 1-4)
- Picture the psalmist reaching out to God, persistent in prayer.

Section 2: Remembering God's Works (Verses 10-15)
- Visualize God's past wonders as a source of hope and trust.

Section 3: God's Path Through the Waters (Verses 16-20)
- Visualize the Red Sea parting, a symbol of God's miraculous guidance.

Summary of Key Images
- Crying out in the night, persistent in prayer.
- Recalling God's mighty deeds as a source of strength.
- Walking on an unseen path through the waters, trusting God's unseen guidance.

Psalm 86: A Prayer for Help and Trust in God's Unfailing Love
Psalm 86 (NRSV):

Incline your ear, O Lord, and answer me, for I am poor and needy. Preserve my life, for I am devoted to you; save your servant who trusts in you. You are my God; be gracious to me, O Lord, for to you do I cry all day long. Gladden the soul of your servant, for to you, O Lord, I lift up my soul. For you, O Lord, are good and forgiving, abounding in steadfast love to all who call on you. Give ear, O Lord, to my prayer; listen to my cry of supplication. In the day of my trouble I call on you, for you will answer me.

There is none like you among the gods, O Lord, nor are there any works like yours. All the nations you have made shall come and bow down before you, O Lord, and shall glorify your name. For you are great and do wondrous things; you alone are God. Teach me your way, O Lord, that I may walk in your truth; give me an undivided heart to revere your name. I give thanks to you, O Lord my God, with my whole heart, and I will glorify your name forever. For great is your steadfast love toward me; you have delivered my soul from the depths of Sheol.

O God, the insolent rise up against me; a band of ruffians seeks my life, and they do not set you before them. But you, O Lord, are a God merciful and gracious, slow to anger and abounding in steadfast love and faithfulness. Turn to me and be gracious to me; give your strength to your servant; save the child of your serving girl. Show me a sign of your favor, so that those who hate me may see it and be put to shame, because you, Lord, have helped me and comforted me.

Reflection:

Psalm 86 is a heartfelt prayer from David, expressing dependence on God in a time of trouble. David cries out with humility, describing himself as "poor and needy," yet filled with trust in God's mercy, love, and faithfulness. Throughout the psalm, David acknowledges God's goodness and greatness, seeking divine guidance and strength to endure his circumstances.

1. A Humble Prayer for Help (Verses 1-7)

The psalm opens with David's plea for God to listen and act. He describes himself as "poor and needy," recognizing his own vulnerability and complete reliance on God. David's request for preservation and joy in verse 4—"gladden the soul of your servant"—shows that even in difficulty, he seeks peace and joy from God alone.

This part of the psalm invites us to approach God with humility, admitting our own need and dependence on His grace. Like David, we can trust that God listens to those who call on Him with a sincere heart.

Related Verse: James 4:10 – "Humble yourselves before the Lord, and he will lift you up."

2. Declaring God's Uniqueness and Seeking His Guidance (Verses 8-13)

In these verses, David shifts from asking for help to praising God's greatness and uniqueness. He declares that there is none like God and envisions a future when all nations will come to worship Him. David then prays for an "undivided heart" to follow God's ways, showing his desire to live with integrity and devotion.

This section reminds us that even in our troubles, worship and gratitude are essential. David's request for an undivided heart challenges us to seek God wholeheartedly, putting aside distractions and remaining focused on His truth.

Related Verse: Proverbs 3:5-6 – "Trust in the Lord with all your heart, and do not rely on your own insight. In all your ways acknowledge him, and he will make straight your paths."

3. Resting in God's Mercy and Faithfulness (Verses 14-17)

David faces threats from those who oppose him, but instead of focusing on his enemies, he turns his heart to God's mercy and faithfulness. He describes God as "merciful and gracious, slow to anger and abounding in steadfast love." David asks for strength and a sign of God's favor, confident that God will ultimately protect and vindicate him.

These final verses remind us to rest in God's character. Even when others oppose us, we can be assured of God's presence, strength, and compassion. David's confidence in God's mercy encourages us to trust Him to handle our battles while we continue to seek His comfort and guidance.

Related Verse: Lamentations 3:22-23 – "The steadfast love of the LORD never ceases, his mercies never come to an end; they are new every morning; great is your faithfulness."

Quote:

"God does not call us to a timid faith, but to a bold, full-hearted dependence on His love and strength." – A.W. Tozer

Application:

This week, make time to come before God with a humble and open heart, bringing your needs and concerns to Him. Like David, seek to develop an undivided heart, focusing on God's truth rather than the distractions or worries around you. Reflect on God's mercy and faithfulness, asking Him to show you how you can grow in trust and surrender to His guidance.

Questions for Reflection:

- Are there areas in my life where I need to trust God more fully?

- How can I focus on God's truth and remain undivided in my devotion to Him?

- In what ways has God shown His mercy and faithfulness to me in the past?

Prayer:

Lord, I come before You as David did, humble and in need of Your help. Give me an undivided heart that seeks You alone, and fill me with the joy of Your presence. I praise You for Your mercy, faithfulness, and steadfast love. Strengthen me in my trials and show me a sign of Your favor, that I may live in confidence and peace. Amen.

Memorization Guide:
Step 1: Break Down Key Sections

1. Verses 1-7: A humble request for God's help and joy.

2. Verses 8-13: A declaration of God's greatness and a request for guidance.

3. Verses 14-17: Trusting in God's mercy and asking for strength.

Step 2: Memorize by Key Themes and Visualizations
Section 1: Humble Plea (Verses 1-7)

- Picture David lifting his voice in prayer, seeking God's help and joy.

Section 2: Worship and Guidance (Verses 8-13)

- Imagine a heart undivided, devoted to God, trusting in His greatness.

Section 3: Assurance in God's Mercy (Verses 14-17)
- Visualize David resting in God's love, confident of His mercy and strength.

Summary of Key Images
- David's humble and sincere plea for God's help.
- Seeking an undivided heart focused on God's truth.
- Trusting in God's mercy, grace, and strength to overcome adversity.

Psalm 91: Dwelling in the Shelter of the Most High
Psalm 91 (NRSV):

You who live in the shelter of the Most High, who abide in the shadow of the Almighty, will say to the Lord, "My refuge and my fortress; my God, in whom I trust." For he will deliver you from the snare of the fowler and from the deadly pestilence; he will cover you with his pinions, and under his wings you will find refuge; his faithfulness is a shield and buckler. You will not fear the terror of the night, or the arrow that flies by day, or the pestilence that stalks in darkness, or the destruction that wastes at noonday.
A thousand may fall at your side, ten thousand at your right hand, but it will not come near you. You will only look with your eyes and see the punishment of the wicked. Because you have made the Lord your refuge, the Most High your dwelling place, no evil shall befall you, no scourge come near your tent. For he will command his angels concerning you to guard you in all your ways. On their hands they will bear you up, so that you will not dash your foot against a stone. You will tread on the lion and the adder, the young lion and the serpent you will trample under foot.
Those who love me, I will deliver; I will protect those who know my name. When they call to me, I will answer them; I will be with them in trouble, I will rescue them and honor them. With long life I will satisfy them, and show them my salvation.

Reflection:

Psalm 91 is one of the most comforting and powerful passages in Scripture, emphasizing God's protection and faithfulness to those who trust in Him. This psalm presents a beautiful promise that those who dwell in the shelter of the Almighty will experience His refuge, strength, and divine protection. This isn't a guarantee of a trouble-free life, but rather a deep assurance of God's presence and deliverance through every trial.

1. Living in God's Shelter (Verses 1-4)

The psalm opens with a declaration of trust and assurance. To "live in the shelter of the Most High" means to abide in God's presence, trusting Him as a refuge. God's protection is likened to a mother bird sheltering her young under her wings. This imagery invites us to see God as a tender protector who covers us with His faithfulness.

This section calls us to make God our dwelling place, relying on His faithfulness in every season. Reflect on how living in God's shelter might change how you approach life's challenges, knowing He is always near.

Related Verse: Isaiah 25:4 – "For you have been a refuge to the poor, a refuge to the needy in their distress, a shelter from the rainstorm and a shade from the heat."

---

2. Assurance Amid Danger (Verses 5-13)

These verses address specific fears—night terrors, arrows, pestilence, and destruction—that God's people may face. The psalmist assures us that no matter how great the danger, those who make God their refuge are secure. The imagery of being guarded by angels and overcoming even fierce animals like lions and snakes symbolizes God's power to protect and strengthen us.

In life, threats can come in many forms, but Psalm 91 encourages us to walk in confidence, knowing that God is greater than any trial. Consider what fears or worries you need to release to God, trusting that He has the power to protect and deliver you.

Related Verse: Proverbs 3:24-26 – "When you lie down, you will not be afraid; when you lie down, your sleep will be sweet. Have no fear of sudden disaster or of the ruin that overtakes the wicked, for the LORD will be at your side and will keep your foot from being snared."

3. God's Promise to Those Who Love Him (Verses 14-16)

The psalm concludes with a powerful promise directly from God. He pledges to deliver, protect, answer, and honor those who love Him. This closing section is both a promise and an invitation to deepen our relationship with God, who desires to be our ultimate protector and savior. It reassures us that God's presence is constant in our lives, through all trouble, and that His love is steadfast.

This is an invitation to find comfort in God's promises and to place our love and trust in Him fully. Reflect on how God's promises encourage you to remain close to Him, seeking Him as your refuge.

Related Verse: John 14:23 – "Jesus replied, 'Anyone who loves me will obey my teaching. My Father will love them, and we will come to them and make our home with them.'"

Quote:

"God's promises are like the stars; the darker the night, the brighter they shine." – David Nicholas

Application:

This week, consider how you can dwell more deeply in God's presence and make Him your true refuge. Identify any areas of fear or worry in your life, and bring them before God, trusting Him as your protector. Let His promises be a source of strength for you. Take time to meditate on God's faithfulness, reminding yourself that He is with you in every circumstance.

Questions for Reflection:
- How can I make God my refuge in both daily life and times of trouble?
- Are there fears or worries I need to release to God's care?
- In what ways have I experienced God's protection and presence in my life?

Prayer:
Lord, thank You for being my refuge and fortress. Help me to live each day in Your presence, trusting in Your faithfulness and power to protect me. Give me courage to release my fears to You and confidence to rest in Your promises. May I love You with all my heart and walk in the assurance of Your salvation. Amen.

Memorization Guide:
Step 1: Break Down Key Sections
1. Verses 1-4: Living in God's shelter and trusting His protection.
2. Verses 5-13: Assurance amid dangers and threats.
3. Verses 14-16: God's promises to those who love and trust Him.

Step 2: Memorize by Key Themes and Visualizations
Section 1: God as Our Shelter (Verses 1-4)
- Visualize a protective shelter and the peace that comes from abiding under God's wings.

Section 2: Divine Protection (Verses 5-13)
- Picture the various threats mentioned, each repelled by God's mighty presence and angelic protection.

Section 3: God's Promises (Verses 14-16)

- Imagine God's comforting voice, pledging deliverance and protection to those who trust Him.

Summary of Key Images
- Dwelling in God's shelter, experiencing His peace and protection.
- Walking confidently in God's protection against every danger.
- Resting in God's personal promises of deliverance and salvation.

Psalm 92: A Song of Praise for God's Faithfulness
Psalm 92 (NRSV):

It is good to give thanks to the Lord, to sing praises to your name, O Most High; to declare your steadfast love in the morning, and your faithfulness by night, to the music of the lute and the harp, to the melody of the lyre. For you, O Lord, have made me glad by your work; at the works of your hands I sing for joy.

How great are your works, O Lord! Your thoughts are very deep! The dullard cannot know, the stupid cannot understand this: though the wicked sprout like grass and all evildoers flourish, they are doomed to destruction forever, but you, O Lord, are on high forever. For your enemies, O Lord, for your enemies shall perish; all evildoers shall be scattered.

But you have exalted my horn like that of the wild ox; you have poured over me fresh oil. My eyes have seen the downfall of my enemies; my ears have heard the doom of my evil assailants. The righteous flourish like the palm tree and grow like a cedar in Lebanon. They are planted in the house of the Lord; they flourish in the courts of our God. In old age they still produce fruit; they are always green and full of sap, showing that the Lord is upright; he is my rock, and there is no unrighteousness in him.

Reflection:

Psalm 92 is a beautiful declaration of praise and thanksgiving, emphasizing God's faithfulness and righteousness. It encourages us to begin and end each day by reflecting on God's goodness, as the psalmist declares God's steadfast love in the morning and His faithfulness at night. This psalm contrasts the fleeting success of the wicked with the lasting strength of the righteous, who, like trees planted in God's presence, continue to thrive and bear fruit throughout their lives.

1. Starting and Ending the Day with Praise (Verses 1-4)

The psalmist opens with the joy of giving thanks to God, proclaiming His love each morning and His faithfulness each night. This rhythm of daily praise fosters an attitude of gratitude and aligns the psalmist's heart with God's goodness. As he reflects on the works of God's hands, he is filled with joy, declaring that it is good to worship the Lord.

This portion of Psalm 92 encourages us to make a habit of praising God daily, reminding ourselves of His faithfulness in every season of life. Reflect on how beginning and ending your day with praise can transform your perspective.

Related Verse: Lamentations 3:22-23 – "The steadfast love of the Lord never ceases; his mercies never come to an end; they are new every morning; great is your faithfulness."

2. The Futility of Wickedness and the Eternal Power of God (Verses 5-11)

Here, the psalmist marvels at the depth of God's wisdom and contrasts it with the short-sightedness of the wicked. He acknowledges that, while evildoers may appear to flourish temporarily, their success is fleeting. The psalmist finds assurance in God's eternal nature, knowing that those who oppose Him will ultimately perish, while God reigns forever.

This passage reminds us to trust in God's eternal justice rather than becoming discouraged by temporary successes of those who act unjustly. God's plans are deep, and His righteousness endures.

Related Verse: Psalm 37:1-2 – "Do not fret because of the wicked; do not be envious of wrongdoers, for they will soon fade like the grass and wither like the green herb."

3. Flourishing Like Trees in God's Presence (Verses 12-15)

The psalm concludes with a beautiful image of the righteous as strong, thriving trees. Like the palm tree and the cedar of Lebanon, which are known for their resilience and longevity, the righteous flourish and remain fruitful even into old age. This flourishing is a result of being "planted in the house of the Lord," rooted in His presence and drawing strength from His faithfulness. These verses encourage us to stay rooted in God, knowing that when we dwell in His presence, we will continue to grow and bear fruit throughout our lives. Our vitality is sustained by God's constant goodness and righteousness.

Related Verse: Jeremiah 17:7-8 – "Blessed is the one who trusts in the Lord, whose confidence is in him. They will be like a tree planted by the water that sends out its roots by the stream. It does not fear when heat comes; its leaves are always green."

Quote:
"Faithfulness in God's presence bears fruit, making us strong and resilient no matter the season." – Anonymous

---

Application:
This week, make it a priority to start and end each day with a moment of praise and thanksgiving to God. Reflect on His steadfast love in the morning and His faithfulness each night. Consider areas in your life where you can deepen your "roots" in God's presence—whether through prayer, reading His Word, or acts of kindness. Ask God to make you like a flourishing tree, bearing fruit throughout all seasons.

Questions for Reflection:
- How can I create a rhythm of daily praise in my life?
- In what ways do I need to trust God's eternal justice over temporary circumstances?

- What steps can I take to deepen my roots in God's presence, allowing me to flourish like the trees in His house?

Prayer:

Lord, thank You for Your steadfast love and faithfulness. Help me to begin and end each day with praise for all You've done. Make me like a tree planted in Your presence, rooted in Your truth, and bearing fruit through all the seasons of life. Let me grow stronger in my faith and trust Your eternal justice. Amen.

Memorization Guide:

Step 1: Break Down Key Sections

1. Verses 1-4: Starting and ending the day with praise for God's love and faithfulness.

2. Verses 5-11: Trusting in God's justice over the fleeting success of the wicked.

3. Verses 12-15: Flourishing like trees planted in God's presence.

Step 2: Memorize by Key Themes and Visualizations

Section 1: Daily Praise (Verses 1-4)
- Picture giving thanks morning and night, celebrating God's steadfast love.

Section 2: God's Justice (Verses 5-11)
- Visualize the temporary "sprouting" of grass versus the eternal strength of God.

Section 3: Flourishing Trees (Verses 12-15)
- Imagine strong trees, thriving and bearing fruit in God's house.

Summary of Key Images
- Starting and ending each day with praise for God's love and faithfulness.
- The contrast between the fleeting success of the wicked and God's eternal justice.
- The righteous flourishing like trees planted in God's presence, bearing fruit in every season.

Psalm 96: Sing a New Song to the Lord
Psalm 96 (NRSV):

O sing to the Lord a new song; sing to the Lord, all the earth. Sing to the Lord, bless his name; tell of his salvation from day to day. Declare his glory among the nations, his marvelous works among all the peoples. For great is the Lord, and greatly to be praised; he is to be revered above all gods. For all the gods of the peoples are idols, but the Lord made the heavens. Honor and majesty are before him; strength and beauty are in his sanctuary.

Ascribe to the Lord, O families of the peoples, ascribe to the Lord glory and strength. Ascribe to the Lord the glory due his name; bring an offering, and come into his courts. Worship the Lord in holy splendor; tremble before him, all the earth.

Say among the nations, "The Lord is king! The world is firmly established; it shall never be moved. He will judge the peoples with equity." Let the heavens be glad, and let the earth rejoice; let the sea roar, and all that fills it; let the field exult, and everything in it. Then shall all the trees of the forest sing for joy before the Lord; for he is coming, for he is coming to judge the earth. He will judge the world with righteousness, and the peoples with his truth.

Reflection:

Psalm 96 is a jubilant call to worship and praise, inviting all creation to declare the greatness of God. It's a celebration of His sovereignty, salvation, and righteous rule over the world. This psalm encourages us to "sing a new song" to the Lord, inviting us to declare His glory not just in our lives but also among the nations. It speaks of the lasting stability God provides as the Creator and the joy of anticipating His righteous judgment.

1. Declaring God's Glory Among the Nations (Verses 1-6)

The psalm opens with a call to "sing a new song" to the Lord, emphasizing a fresh and ongoing proclamation of God's salvation. The psalmist urges us to bless God's name and declare His marvelous works, reminding us that the Lord is to be praised above all else. While idols are empty, God is the Creator of the heavens, surrounded by honor and majesty.

This section challenges us to make our lives a testimony to God's greatness, using every opportunity to share His goodness and power with others. Reflect on how your words, actions, and attitudes can declare God's glory daily.

Related Verse: Matthew 5:16 – "In the same way, let your light shine before others, so that they may see your good works and give glory to your Father in heaven."

2. Worshiping in the Splendor of Holiness (Verses 7-9)

The psalmist invites all people to ascribe glory and strength to God, acknowledging His majesty. Worship is described as something to be approached with reverence and awe, recognizing God's holy splendor. The image of bringing an offering and coming into God's courts highlights the importance of approaching Him with a heart of humility and gratitude.

This passage reminds us to enter God's presence with reverence, setting aside distractions and focusing solely on His greatness. Think about how you can incorporate a sense of holy reverence into your times of worship and prayer.

Related Verse: Hebrews 12:28-29 – "Therefore, since we are receiving a kingdom that cannot be shaken, let us be thankful, and so worship God acceptably with reverence and awe, for our 'God is a consuming fire.'"

3. Rejoicing in God's Righteous Rule (Verses 10-13)

The psalm ends with a vision of creation rejoicing in anticipation of God's coming judgment. The nations, the heavens, the earth, the sea, and all its creatures are called to celebrate because the Lord is coming to judge the world with righteousness. This depiction of nature's joy and the steadfastness of God's rule brings hope and reassurance to the faithful.

This part of the psalm encourages us to rejoice in God's righteous justice, which brings ultimate peace and restoration to the world. Consider how trusting in God's justice can bring you peace, even in uncertain times, knowing that He will judge with equity and truth.

Related Verse: Revelation 21:4 – "He will wipe every tear from their eyes. There will be no more death or mourning or crying or pain, for the old order of things has passed away."

Quote:
"Worship is the highest and noblest activity of which man, by the grace of God, is capable." – John Stott

Application:
This week, focus on ways you can declare God's greatness in your daily interactions. Start your day with worship, intentionally praising God for His faithfulness and salvation. In your conversations, find natural ways to reflect God's love and goodness to others. Let your life be a new song, bringing glory to God and pointing others to His truth.

Questions for Reflection:
- How can I declare God's glory in my daily life, not just in words but in actions?
- Do I approach worship with a sense of reverence and awe, recognizing God's holiness?

- How does trusting in God's righteous judgment bring peace and joy to my heart?

Prayer:
Lord, thank You for Your majesty and for inviting us to worship You. Help me to live each day as a testimony to Your greatness, sharing Your love and truth with others. Let my worship come from a place of reverence and awe, honoring You as the King of all. May all creation sing for joy, and may my heart rejoice in Your coming righteousness and justice. Amen.

Memorization Guide:

Step 1: Break Down Key Sections

1. Verses 1-6: Declaring God's glory and greatness among the nations.
2. Verses 7-9: Worshiping with reverence, ascribing glory and strength to God.
3. Verses 10-13: Rejoicing in God's righteous rule and His coming judgment.

Step 2: Memorize by Key Themes and Visualizations

Section 1: Declaring God's Glory (Verses 1-6)
- Picture the world singing praises and proclaiming God's works.

Section 2: Worshiping in Reverence (Verses 7-9)
- Visualize coming into God's presence with a heart of awe and offering.

Section 3: Joy in God's Judgment (Verses 10-13)
- Imagine all creation—heavens, earth, and sea—rejoicing in anticipation of God's righteous rule.

Summary of Key Images
- Singing a new song, sharing God's salvation and marvelous works.
- Worshiping with reverence, recognizing God's holiness.
- Creation rejoicing in God's righteous judgment and steadfast rule.

Psalm 100: Enter His Gates with Thanksgiving
Psalm 100 (NRSV):

Make a joyful noise to the Lord, all the earth. Worship the Lord with gladness; come into his presence with singing. Know that the Lord is God. It is he that made us, and we are his; we are his people, and the sheep of his pasture. Enter his gates with thanksgiving, and his courts with praise. Give thanks to him, bless his name. For the Lord is good; his steadfast love endures forever, and his faithfulness to all generations.

Reflection:

Psalm 100 is a timeless call to worship and thanksgiving, filled with joy and reverence. This brief but powerful psalm invites us to approach God with gladness, acknowledging Him as our Creator and Shepherd. Each verse overflows with gratitude, celebrating God's goodness, love, and faithfulness. It reminds us that worship is both a joyful response and a humble recognition of who God is.

1. A Call to Joyful Worship (Verses 1-2)

The psalm opens with a universal call to worship: "Make a joyful noise to the Lord, all the earth." This invitation emphasizes that worship is meant to be filled with joy, gladness, and song. Approaching God with singing reflects an attitude of gratitude and delight in His presence.

These verses encourage us to make joy and gratitude the foundation of our worship. Reflect on how you can approach God with a heart of gladness, allowing worship to be a celebration of His goodness.

Related Verse: Philippians 4:4 – "Rejoice in the Lord always; again I will say, Rejoice."

---

2. Knowing Our Identity in God (Verse 3)

In this verse, the psalmist reminds us of two essential truths: that God is our Creator and that we belong to Him. "Know that the Lord is God; it is he that made us, and we are his." This simple declaration gives us confidence in our identity as His people, the "sheep of his pasture." God's ownership over us is not just one of authority but of tender care, like a shepherd who knows, leads, and protects his flock.

This verse challenges us to embrace our identity as God's beloved people, recognizing that He created us and guides us faithfully. Consider how understanding your place as one of God's "sheep" can deepen your trust and peace in His care.

Related Verse: John 10:14 – "I am the good shepherd. I know my own and my own know me."

3. Thanksgiving and Praise in God's Presence (Verses 4-5)

The psalmist invites us to "enter his gates with thanksgiving, and his courts with praise." Thanksgiving is not only an expression of gratitude but a way of entering into God's presence. We are encouraged to "bless his name," acknowledging His goodness, steadfast love, and enduring faithfulness to all generations.

This section reminds us that gratitude is central to worship, and it is the doorway through which we encounter God's presence. Reflect on how incorporating thanksgiving into your daily routine can shift your perspective, bringing you closer to God and helping you recognize His goodness in your life.

Related Verse: Colossians 3:17 – "And whatever you do, in word or deed, do everything in the name of the Lord Jesus, giving thanks to God the Father through him."

Quote:
"Gratitude is the most exquisite form of courtesy, a recognition

that we are constantly blessed." – Henri Nouwen

Application:

This week, make a conscious effort to begin and end each day with thanksgiving. Take a few moments each morning to thank God for who He is, and each evening to thank Him for His faithfulness throughout the day. Allow gratitude to shape your perspective, even in challenges, trusting that God is good and faithful. In your worship, let your heart overflow with joy and gladness, celebrating the love and care of your Creator and Shepherd.

Questions for Reflection:

- How can I bring more joy and gladness into my worship?
- Do I live each day with an awareness of my identity as God's beloved and cared-for child?
- What are specific ways I can practice thanksgiving daily to stay close to God?

Prayer:

Lord, I come into Your presence with joy and thanksgiving. Thank You for being my Creator, my Shepherd, and my faithful God. Help me to live each day with gratitude, recognizing Your goodness in every moment. Let my worship be filled with gladness and my heart with thanksgiving, for Your steadfast love endures forever. Amen.

Memorization Guide:

Step 1: Break Down Key Sections

1. Verses 1-2: A call to joyful worship and gladness.
2. Verse 3: Recognizing God as Creator and embracing our identity as His people.

3. Verses 4-5: Entering with thanksgiving, acknowledging God's goodness, love, and faithfulness.

Step 2: Memorize by Key Themes and Visualizations

Section 1: Joyful Worship (Verses 1-2)
- Picture a joyful gathering, celebrating and singing to God with gladness.

Section 2: Our Identity in God (Verse 3)
- Visualize God as our Shepherd and ourselves as His flock, resting in His care.

Section 3: Thanksgiving and Praise (Verses 4-5)
- Imagine entering God's presence with gratitude, celebrating His love and faithfulness.

Summary of Key Images
- Joyful, glad-hearted worship before God.
- Trust in our identity as God's beloved people, guided by Him as our Shepherd.
- Entering God's presence with thanksgiving, acknowledging His goodness and love.

Psalm 103: Bless the Lord, O My Soul
Psalm 103 (NRSV):

Bless the Lord, O my soul, and all that is within me, bless his holy name. Bless the Lord, O my soul, and do not forget all his benefits—who forgives all your iniquity, who heals all your diseases, who redeems your life from the Pit, who crowns you with steadfast love and mercy, who satisfies you with good as long as you live so that your youth is renewed like the eagle's. The Lord works vindication and justice for all who are oppressed. He made known his ways to Moses, his acts to the people of Israel. The Lord is merciful and gracious, slow to anger and abounding in steadfast love. He will not always accuse, nor will he keep his anger forever. He does not deal with us according to our sins, nor repay us according to our iniquities. For as the heavens are high above the earth, so great is his steadfast love toward those who fear him; as far as the east is from the west, so far he removes our transgressions from us.

As a father has compassion for his children, so the Lord has compassion for those who fear him. For he knows how we were made; he remembers that we are dust. As for mortals, their days are like grass; they flourish like a flower of the field; for the wind passes over it, and it is gone, and its place knows it no more. But the steadfast love of the Lord is from everlasting to everlasting on those who fear him, and his righteousness to children's children, to those who keep his covenant and remember to do his commandments.

The Lord has established his throne in the heavens, and his kingdom rules over all. Bless the Lord, O you his angels, you mighty ones who do his bidding, obedient to his spoken word. Bless the Lord, all his hosts, his ministers that do his will. Bless the Lord, all his works, in all places of his dominion. Bless the Lord, O my soul.

Reflection:
Psalm 103 is a profound expression of gratitude and worship, celebrating God's compassion, mercy, and enduring love. The psalmist begins by instructing his soul to "bless the Lord" and reminds himself to "not forget all his benefits." Through the vivid descriptions of God's forgiveness, healing, and compassion, this psalm is a beautiful reminder of who God is and what He does for His people. The emphasis on God's mercy, steadfast love, and kindness lifts our eyes from earthly concerns to the eternal faithfulness of our Creator.

1. Remembering God's Benefits (Verses 1-5)
The psalm opens with an exhortation to "bless the Lord" with everything within us, acknowledging all of God's benefits. The psalmist recounts specific blessings: forgiveness, healing, redemption, love, and renewal. These verses remind us that God not only forgives but also fills our lives with good things, renewing our strength and restoring our spirits.

Reflect on the "benefits" God has given you, from spiritual blessings like forgiveness to daily provisions. Consider how remembering these gifts can foster a heart of gratitude and praise.

Related Verse: Ephesians 1:3 – "Blessed be the God and Father of our Lord Jesus Christ, who has blessed us in Christ with every spiritual blessing in the heavenly places."

2. Celebrating God's Compassion and Forgiveness (Verses 6-14)
In this section, the psalmist shifts to a reflection on God's mercy and compassion. God is described as "merciful and gracious, slow to anger and abounding in steadfast love." He does not treat us as our sins deserve but removes our transgressions "as far

as the east is from the west." This imagery portrays God's profound forgiveness and love toward those who seek Him. These verses invite us to celebrate the depth of God's mercy, understanding that His compassion is endless. Reflect on how God's grace has impacted your life, forgiving your sins and healing your heart.

Related Verse: Lamentations 3:22-23 – "The steadfast love of the LORD never ceases; his mercies never come to an end; they are new every morning; great is your faithfulness."

3. God's Everlasting Love and Faithfulness (Verses 15-22)

The psalm concludes with a contrast between human frailty and God's eternal love. While human life is fleeting, God's love is "from everlasting to everlasting." The psalmist reminds us that God's kingdom rules over all, and he invites all of creation—angels, hosts, and all His works—to join in blessing the Lord. This section calls us to see God's love as unchanging and boundless, stretching across generations and enduring forever. Reflect on the steadfastness of God's love in your life and how His eternal perspective brings hope and assurance, even in uncertain times.

Related Verse: Isaiah 40:8 – "The grass withers, the flower fades; but the word of our God will stand forever."

Quote:

"Gratitude is the memory of the heart." – Jean-Baptiste Massieu

Application:

This week, make it a priority to "bless the Lord" by consciously remembering and giving thanks for His benefits. Write down specific ways God has shown you forgiveness, compassion, and provision, both in the past and present. Let this gratitude shape your interactions and perspective, and make an intentional effort to share one of God's "benefits" with someone in need, whether through encouragement, support, or an act of kindness.

Questions for Reflection:
- What are some specific "benefits" I've received from God that I can celebrate this week?
- How has God shown His compassion and forgiveness in my life?
- In what ways can I live with an awareness of God's everlasting love, sharing it with others?

Prayer:

Lord, thank You for Your abundant blessings and boundless love. Help me to remember all the ways You have forgiven, healed, and renewed me. Let my soul continually bless Your name, celebrating Your goodness and compassion. Thank You for being merciful and faithful, from generation to generation. May my life reflect gratitude for all You have done. Amen.

Memorization Guide:

Step 1: Break Down Key Sections
1. Verses 1-5: Remembering and blessing God for His many benefits.
2. Verses 6-14: Celebrating God's mercy, compassion, and forgiveness.
3. Verses 15-22: Embracing God's everlasting love and inviting all creation to praise Him.

Step 2: Memorize by Key Themes and Visualizations

Section 1: Blessing God for His Benefits (Verses 1-5)

- Picture a heart full of gratitude, overflowing with praise for God's kindness.

Section 2: Compassion and Forgiveness (Verses 6-14)
- Visualize God removing sins "as far as the east is from the west," a symbol of His boundless mercy.

Section 3: Everlasting Love (Verses 15-22)
- Imagine all creation joining together in praise, united by God's eternal love.

Summary of Key Images

- Blessing God for His "benefits"—forgiveness, healing, love, and renewal.
- Celebrating God's compassion, removing our sins and showing deep mercy.
- Embracing God's everlasting love, an unchanging promise across all generations.

Psalm 104: Celebrating the Creator's Majesty and Provision
Psalm 104 (NRSV):

Bless the Lord, O my soul. O Lord my God, you are very great. You are clothed with honor and majesty, wrapped in light as with a garment. You stretch out the heavens like a tent, you set the beams of your chambers on the waters, you make the clouds your chariot, you ride on the wings of the wind, you make the winds your messengers, fire and flame your ministers.

You set the earth on its foundations, so that it shall never be shaken. You cover it with the deep as with a garment; the waters stood above the mountains. At your rebuke they flee; at the sound of your thunder they take to flight. They rose up to the mountains, ran down to the valleys to the place that you appointed for them. You set a boundary that they may not pass, so that they might not again cover the earth.

You make springs gush forth in the valleys; they flow between the hills, giving drink to every wild animal; the wild asses quench their thirst. By the streams the birds of the air have their habitation; they sing among the branches. From your lofty abode you water the mountains; the earth is satisfied with the fruit of your work.

You cause the grass to grow for the cattle, and plants for people to use, to bring forth food from the earth, and wine to gladden the human heart, oil to make the face shine, and bread to strengthen the human heart. The trees of the Lord are watered abundantly, the cedars of Lebanon that he planted. In them the birds build their nests; the stork has its home in the fir trees. The high mountains are for the wild goats; the rocks are a refuge for the coneys.

You have made the moon to mark the seasons; the sun knows its time for setting. You make darkness, and it is night, when all the animals of the forest come creeping out. The young lions roar for their prey, seeking their food from God. When the sun rises, they withdraw and lie down in their dens. People go out to their work and to their labor until the evening.

O Lord, how manifold are your works! In wisdom you have made them all; the earth is full of your creatures. Yonder is the sea, great and wide, creeping things innumerable are there, living things both small and great. There go the ships, and Leviathan that you formed to sport in it.

These all look to you to give them their food in due season; when you give to them, they gather it up; when you open your hand, they are filled with good things. When you hide your face, they are dismayed; when you take away their breath, they die and return to their dust. When you send forth your spirit, they are created, and you renew the face of the ground.

May the glory of the Lord endure forever; may the Lord rejoice in his works—who looks on the earth and it trembles, who touches the mountains and they smoke. I will sing to the Lord as long as I live; I will sing praise to my God while I have being. May my meditation be pleasing to him, for I rejoice in the Lord. Let sinners be consumed from the earth, and let the wicked be no more. Bless the Lord, O my soul. Praise the Lord!

Reflection:

Psalm 104 is a magnificent celebration of God as Creator and Sustainer. This psalm captures God's power and presence throughout creation, from the heavens stretched out like a tent to the creatures of the earth. The psalmist marvels at how each element of nature, from mountains to streams to animals, reflects God's glory and wisdom. This psalm invites us to stand in awe of God's handiwork and to see His intimate care in every aspect of the natural world.

1. Marveling at God's Majesty (Verses 1-4)

The psalm opens with the psalmist blessing God and proclaiming His greatness. God's majesty is seen in the heavens, which He stretches out, and in the winds, which carry His presence. This imagery presents God as transcendent yet present, powerfully moving through all creation.

This section encourages us to take time to recognize the beauty and majesty of God, to see His handiwork in the vastness of the sky, and to remember that all creation is under His command.

Related Verse: Isaiah 40:22 – "It is he who sits above the circle of the earth, and its inhabitants are like grasshoppers; who stretches out the heavens like a curtain, and spreads them like a tent to live in."

2. God's Provision in Nature (Verses 5-18)

These verses describe God's provision for the earth, from setting boundaries for the seas to watering the mountains and feeding the animals. The springs, grass, and trees are all provided for by God's hand, creating a delicate balance that sustains life.

Reflect on how God's provision is evident in nature, meeting the needs of every creature. This passage invites us to recognize God as our Provider, who cares for all creation with wisdom and generosity.

Related Verse: Matthew 6:26 – "Look at the birds of the air; they neither sow nor reap nor gather into barns, and yet your heavenly Father feeds them. Are you not of more value than they?"

3. Creation's Rhythm and Our Dependence on God (Verses 19-30)

The psalmist highlights the rhythms of creation—the moon

marking seasons, the sun rising and setting. These natural rhythms remind us of our dependence on God, as all creatures, great and small, rely on Him for sustenance and life. The psalmist notes that when God's Spirit is sent forth, life is renewed, but when God withdraws, life returns to dust.

These verses encourage us to trust in God's timing and provision, knowing that He sustains us each day. Reflect on the natural rhythms in your own life that remind you of your dependence on God's presence and provision.

Related Verse: Acts 17:28 – "For in him we live and move and have our being."

4. Rejoicing in God's Glory (Verses 31-35)

The psalm concludes with a prayer for God's glory to endure forever, and a personal vow to praise God as long as the psalmist lives. There is joy in celebrating God's creation and rejoicing in the Lord's enduring presence and power. The psalmist's meditation and praise reflect a heart fully devoted to God, filled with awe and gratitude.

This final section encourages us to live in constant worship, marveling at God's works and allowing our lives to be a reflection of His glory. Take time each day to praise God for His creation and to let gratitude shape your meditation and actions.

Related Verse: Revelation 4:11 – "You are worthy, our Lord and God, to receive glory and honor and power, for you created all things, and by your will they existed and were created."

Quote:

"Creation is a canvas painted by God, inviting us to wonder and worship the Artist behind it all." – Anonymous

Application:

This week, set aside time to appreciate God's creation. Take a walk outdoors, observe the beauty around you, and give thanks for God's provision. Consider how each element of nature reflects God's care and creativity. Let this appreciation deepen your worship, knowing that the same God who provides for nature also sustains and cares for you.

Questions for Reflection:
- How does observing creation help me appreciate God's character and power?
- In what ways can I trust in God's provision, knowing He sustains all things?
- How can I incorporate gratitude and worship for God's creation into my daily life?

Prayer:
Lord, thank You for the beauty and majesty of Your creation. Help me to see Your hand in every part of nature, from the heavens to the smallest creatures. Teach me to trust in Your provision and to live with a heart full of gratitude for all You have made. May my life be a reflection of Your glory, and may my soul always bless Your name. Amen.

Memorization Guide:
Step 1: Break Down Key Sections
1. Verses 1-4: Marveling at God's majesty and presence in creation.
2. Verses 5-18: Recognizing God's provision in nature.
3. Verses 19-30: Acknowledging creation's rhythms and our dependence on God.

4. Verses 31-35: Rejoicing in God's glory and enduring praise.

Step 2: Memorize by Key Themes and Visualizations

Section 1: God's Majesty (Verses 1-4)
- Visualize the heavens stretched out like a tent, filled with God's light and power.

Section 2: Provision in Nature (Verses 5-18)
- Picture the earth and creatures flourishing through God's provision, from springs to trees to animals.

Section 3: Rhythms of Creation (Verses 19-30)
- Imagine the sun and moon setting, the natural cycles that all reflect God's sustaining power.

Section 4: Eternal Praise (Verses 31-35)
- Visualize the psalmist singing praise, rejoicing in God's glory and presence throughout creation.

Summary of Key Images

- God's majesty displayed in creation's vastness and beauty.
- His provision and care for all living things, sustaining life.
- The rhythm of creation, reflecting our dependence on God.
- A heart rejoicing in God's glory, living in constant praise.

Psalm 111: Praising God's Great Works and Faithfulness

Psalm 111 (NRSV):

Praise the Lord! I will give thanks to the Lord with my whole heart, in the company of the upright, in the congregation. Great are the works of the Lord, studied by all who delight in them. Full of honor and majesty is his work, and his righteousness endures forever. He has gained renown by his wonderful deeds; the Lord is gracious and merciful. He provides food for those who fear him; he is ever mindful of his covenant.

He has shown his people the power of his works, in giving them the heritage of the nations. The works of his hands are faithful and just; all his precepts are trustworthy. They are established forever and ever, to be performed with faithfulness and uprightness. He sent redemption to his people; he has commanded his covenant forever. Holy and awesome is his name. The fear of the Lord is the beginning of wisdom; all those who practice it have a good understanding. His praise endures forever.

Reflection:

Psalm 111 is a beautiful declaration of praise for God's mighty works, His faithfulness, and His enduring covenant with His people. The psalmist begins with a vow to praise God "with my whole heart," expressing gratitude not only in solitude but also among the community of believers. Through a recounting of God's righteous acts and steadfast love, the psalm highlights God's compassion, justice, and the importance of fearing the Lord.

1. Wholehearted Praise in Community (Verse 1)

The psalm opens with a commitment to praise the Lord with "my whole heart." This is not half-hearted or reserved worship, but a declaration of complete gratitude. The psalmist also chooses to give thanks "in the company of the upright, in the congregation," recognizing the value of communal praise. Reflect on the importance of worshiping God both privately and with others. How can you incorporate wholehearted praise into your life, and how might sharing this with a community of faith strengthen your walk with God?

Related Verse: Hebrews 10:24-25 – "And let us consider how to stir up one another to love and good works, not neglecting to meet together, as is the habit of some, but encouraging one another, and all the more as you see the Day drawing near."

2. Meditating on God's Majestic Works (Verses 2-4)

The psalmist speaks of God's works as "great," "full of honor and majesty," and "studied by all who delight in them." This verse reminds us to be in awe of God's deeds and to take time to study and reflect on what He has done. The psalmist goes on to acknowledge God's mercy and graciousness, declaring that He is worthy of our praise.

These verses encourage us to intentionally meditate on God's actions, His creation, and His kindness toward us. Reflect on specific "great works" God has done in your life, and consider how taking time to study them can deepen your appreciation for His mercy and faithfulness.

Related Verse: Psalm 77:11-12 – "I will remember the deeds of the LORD; yes, I will remember your wonders of old. I will ponder all your work, and meditate on your mighty deeds."

3. Faithful Provision and Covenant-Keeping (Verses 5-9)

The psalmist continues by celebrating God's provision, emphasizing that He "provides food for those who fear him" and is "ever mindful of his covenant." God's faithfulness is evident in

His works, which are "faithful and just." He has redeemed His people, showcasing His steadfast commitment to His covenant. These verses remind us that God provides for our needs and fulfills His promises. God's covenant is unbreakable, and His redemption brings us hope. Reflect on ways that God has provided for you, and take comfort in His promise to remain faithful.

Related Verse: Philippians 4:19 – "And my God will supply every need of yours according to his riches in glory in Christ Jesus."

4. The Fear of the Lord and the Foundation of Wisdom (Verse 10)

The psalm concludes with the powerful statement, "The fear of the Lord is the beginning of wisdom." This reverent respect for God is the foundation of true understanding and wisdom. The psalmist declares that practicing this "fear of the Lord" is essential for a life that aligns with God's will.

This verse calls us to embrace a holy respect and reverence for God. Reflect on how deepening your respect for God's holiness and authority can enhance your wisdom, strengthen your walk, and deepen your faith.

Related Verse: Proverbs 9:10 – "The fear of the LORD is the beginning of wisdom, and the knowledge of the Holy One is insight."

Quote:
"True wisdom is found in reverence for God, for it places us in the right posture before our Creator." – Charles Spurgeon

Application:
This week, commit to praising God wholeheartedly, both privately and within your community. Take time to study and

meditate on God's works in your life and around you, recognizing His provision and faithfulness. Ask God to deepen your understanding of His majesty and holiness, and seek to cultivate a heart that reveres and respects Him above all else. Let this "fear of the Lord" be the foundation of your wisdom and a source of joy.

Questions for Reflection:
- How can I bring wholehearted praise into my daily life?
- What "great works" of God can I meditate on this week to increase my gratitude?
- How does respecting God's holiness influence my decisions and actions?

Prayer:
Lord, I thank You for Your great and wondrous works. You are faithful and just, and Your love endures forever. Help me to praise You wholeheartedly, to meditate on Your kindness, and to revere You as the source of all wisdom. Teach me to live with respect for Your holiness, allowing Your truth to guide my heart and mind. Amen.

Memorization Guide:
Step 1: Break Down Key Sections
1. Verse 1: Wholehearted praise, both personally and in community.
2. Verses 2-4: Meditating on God's great and gracious works.
3. Verses 5-9: Celebrating God's faithful provision and covenant.
4. Verse 10: Embracing the fear of the Lord as the foundation of wisdom.

Step 2: Memorize by Key Themes and Visualizations

Section 1: Wholehearted Praise (Verse 1)
- Visualize yourself praising God with joy, surrounded by a community of faith.

Section 2: Meditating on God's Works (Verses 2-4)
- Picture God's majesty in creation and acts of mercy, reminding yourself of His goodness.

Section 3: Faithfulness and Covenant (Verses 5-9)
- Imagine God's steady provision and redemption, comforting His people with faithfulness.

Section 4: The Fear of the Lord (Verse 10)
- Visualize standing in reverence before God, acknowledging Him as the source of wisdom.

Summary of Key Images
- Wholehearted, joyful praise both in solitude and with a community of faith.
- Reflecting on God's wondrous works, filled with majesty and grace.
- Trusting in God's faithful provision and commitment to His covenant.
- Embracing the fear of the Lord as the beginning of wisdom and true understanding.

Psalm 112: The Blessed Life of the Righteous
Psalm 112 (NRSV):

Praise the Lord! Happy are those who fear the Lord, who greatly delight in his commandments. Their descendants will be mighty in the land; the generation of the upright will be blessed. Wealth and riches are in their houses, and their righteousness endures forever. They rise in the darkness as a light for the upright; they are gracious, merciful, and righteous.

It is well with those who deal generously and lend, who conduct their affairs with justice. For the righteous will never be moved; they will be remembered forever. They are not afraid of evil tidings; their hearts are firm, secure in the Lord. Their hearts are steady; they will not be afraid; in the end they will look in triumph on their foes.

They have distributed freely, they have given to the poor; their righteousness endures forever; their horn is exalted in honor. The wicked see it and are angry; they gnash their teeth and melt away; the desire of the wicked comes to nothing.

Reflection:

Psalm 112 is a beautiful picture of the life of a person who fears the Lord and lives righteously. It outlines the blessings, security, and impact of a life lived in alignment with God's will. Those who delight in God's commandments are promised strength, peace, and lasting influence. The psalm highlights the importance of generosity, justice, and unwavering trust in God, contrasting the security of the righteous with the instability of the wicked.

1. Delighting in God's Commandments (Verse 1)

The psalm opens with praise and the assurance of happiness for those who fear the Lord and delight in His commandments. This delight isn't merely about following rules but about embracing God's ways with joy and reverence, understanding that His commandments bring life and wisdom.

Reflect on how delighting in God's commandments might deepen your relationship with Him. Consider how embracing His ways can transform your heart and bring true joy.

Related Verse: Psalm 1:2 – "But their delight is in the law of the LORD, and on his law they meditate day and night."

---

2. Strength, Light, and Security for the Righteous (Verses 2-8)

The psalmist describes the blessings of the righteous, including a strong legacy, wealth, and enduring righteousness. The righteous are compared to a light rising in darkness, bringing grace, mercy, and justice. They are described as immovable, unshaken even by "evil tidings," because their hearts are secure in the Lord.

These verses invite us to trust in God's provision and strength, knowing that righteousness brings a secure foundation. Reflect on how trusting God's promises can help you stay unafraid, even in challenging situations.

Related Verse: Proverbs 10:30 – "The righteous will never be removed, but the wicked will not dwell in the land."

---

3. Generosity and Lasting Influence (Verses 9-10)

The righteous are generous, freely giving to those in need. Their actions bring lasting honor and reflect God's heart of compassion. The psalm closes by contrasting the joy and security of the righteous with the frustration of the wicked, whose desires will ultimately come to nothing.

This section encourages us to live generously, knowing that kindness and giving to others create a lasting legacy. Reflect on how you can incorporate generosity into your life as a testament to God's goodness.

Related Verse: 2 Corinthians 9:9 – "As it is written, 'They have freely scattered their gifts to the poor; their righteousness endures forever.'"

Quote:
"Generosity is giving more than you can, and pride is taking less than you need." – Kahlil Gibran

---

Application:
This week, focus on how you can embrace God's commandments with joy, seeing them as guidance for a life of wisdom and security. Reflect on any fears or insecurities, and bring them to God, asking Him to strengthen your heart. Consider practical ways to demonstrate generosity, sharing what you have to bless others and build a lasting legacy of kindness and love.

Questions for Reflection:
- Do I truly delight in God's commandments, seeing them as a source of joy and wisdom?
- In what ways can I strengthen my trust in God to remain steady in challenging times?
- How can I live a life of generosity, sharing what God has blessed me with to support others?

Prayer:
Lord, thank You for the blessings that come from fearing You and walking in Your ways. Help me to delight in Your commandments and to trust in Your promises. May my life be filled with generosity, reflecting Your grace and love. Strengthen my heart to remain steady, secure in Your presence, and unshaken by life's challenges. Amen.

Memorization Guide:

Step 1: Break Down Key Sections
1. Verse 1: Delighting in God's commandments and the blessings of those who fear Him.

2. Verses 2-8: The strength, light, and security of the righteous.

3. Verses 9-10: Generosity and the enduring legacy of the righteous.

Step 2: Memorize by Key Themes and Visualizations

Section 1: Delighting in God's Commandments (Verse 1)
- Visualize embracing God's commandments with joy, knowing they bring wisdom and life.

Section 2: Security in the Lord (Verses 2-8)
- Picture a strong, immovable light shining in darkness, representing the stability and grace of the righteous.

Section 3: Generosity and Legacy (Verses 9-10)
- Imagine the act of giving freely, bringing joy to others and creating a lasting impact.

Summary of Key Images
- Joyfully embracing God's commandments as a source of life and guidance.

- The unshakable strength and security of the righteous, even in challenging times.

- Living generously and creating a legacy that reflects God's compassion and love.

Psalm 113: Praise the Lord Who Raises the Lowly
Psalm 113 (NRSV):

Praise the Lord! Praise, O servants of the Lord; praise the name of the Lord. Blessed be the name of the Lord from this time on and forevermore. From the rising of the sun to its setting, the name of the Lord is to be praised. The Lord is high above all nations, and his glory above the heavens.

Who is like the Lord our God, who is seated on high, who looks far down on the heavens and the earth? He raises the poor from the dust, and lifts the needy from the ash heap, to make them sit with princes, with the princes of his people. He gives the barren woman a home, making her the joyous mother of children. Praise the Lord!

Reflection:

Psalm 113 is a psalm of pure praise, exalting God as the One who is high above all and yet compassionate toward the lowly. The psalmist calls us to praise the Lord from "the rising of the sun to its setting," affirming that God's greatness is eternal. This psalm celebrates God's mercy and justice, reminding us that He notices those society overlooks, lifting them up and restoring their dignity.

1. Praising God's Name Forever (Verses 1-3)

The psalm opens with a call for continual praise, blessing the name of the Lord forever. The praise is not confined to one place or time but is ongoing, from morning to night. God's name is holy and deserving of unending reverence from His people. These verses encourage us to make praise a constant part of our lives, recognizing God's worthiness at all times. Reflect on how beginning and ending each day with praise can transform your perspective and deepen your connection with God.

Related Verse: Psalm 34:1 – "I will bless the Lord at all times; his praise shall continually be in my mouth."

2. God's Exalted Position and Compassion (Verses 4-6)

The psalmist describes the Lord as "high above all nations," whose glory reaches above the heavens. Despite His exalted position, God humbles Himself to see the needs of the earth. This divine humility demonstrates God's compassion and His attentiveness to His creation, even though He reigns in majesty. This section reminds us of the awe-inspiring fact that the Creator of the universe cares deeply about the lives of His people. Reflect on how God's greatness and His compassion can coexist, and how this knowledge brings comfort in times of need.
Related Verse: Isaiah 57:15 – "For thus says the high and lofty one who inhabits eternity, whose name is Holy: I dwell in the high and holy place, and also with those who are contrite and humble in spirit."

3. Raising the Lowly and Restoring Joy (Verses 7-9)

The psalm concludes with a picture of God's justice and mercy as He lifts the poor from the dust and raises the needy from the ash heap. God transforms the lives of the lowly, seating them with princes and providing a home for the barren woman, giving her joy and fulfillment. This powerful image reflects God's heart for the marginalized and His desire to bring restoration and dignity.
These verses remind us that God is not only aware of suffering but actively works to uplift and restore those who are overlooked. Consider how you can reflect God's compassion by showing kindness to those who feel abandoned or forgotten.
Related Verse: 1 Samuel 2:8 – "He raises up the poor from the dust; he lifts the needy from the ash heap, to make them sit with

princes and inherit a seat of honor."

Quote:
"God is most glorified in us when we are most satisfied in Him." – John Piper

Application:
This week, make a conscious effort to praise God throughout the day, from the moment you wake up to the time you go to sleep. Take time to reflect on His greatness, remembering that He is both majestic and compassionate. Look for opportunities to lift others up, whether through words of encouragement, acts of kindness, or listening with compassion. In doing so, you can reflect God's heart for the lowly and His desire to restore dignity to all people.

Questions for Reflection:
- How can I incorporate praise into my daily routine, recognizing God's worthiness at all times?
- What does it mean to me that God, who is above all, cares deeply for each individual?
- In what ways can I lift others up, reflecting God's compassion for the lowly?

Prayer:
Lord, thank You for Your greatness and Your compassion. You are high above all, yet You see me and know my needs. Help me to live with a heart full of praise, honoring You from morning to night. Give me opportunities to uplift others and to reflect Your love and mercy to those who need it. Thank You for Your unending faithfulness and for restoring joy to those who are lowly. Amen.

Memorization Guide:
Step 1: Break Down Key Sections
1. Verses 1-3: Praising God's name continually, from morning to night.

2. Verses 4-6: Recognizing God's exalted position and His compassionate humility.

3. Verses 7-9: Celebrating God's mercy in raising the lowly and restoring joy.

Step 2: Memorize by Key Themes and Visualizations
Section 1: Continual Praise (Verses 1-3)
- Visualize lifting up praise to God from dawn to dusk, reflecting His worthiness throughout the day.

Section 2: God's Majesty and Compassion (Verses 4-6)
- Picture God seated above the heavens yet humbling Himself to be close to those in need.

Section 3: Raising the Lowly (Verses 7-9)
- Imagine God lifting the poor from the dust, bringing dignity and joy to the marginalized.

Summary of Key Images
- Unceasing praise for God's name, from sunrise to sunset.
- God's exalted position balanced with His deep compassion for humanity.
- The transformation of the lowly, lifted by God's mercy and restored to joy.

Psalm 118: His Steadfast Love Endures Forever
Psalm 118 (NRSV):

O give thanks to the Lord, for he is good; his steadfast love endures forever! Let Israel say, "His steadfast love endures forever." Let the house of Aaron say, "His steadfast love endures forever." Let those who fear the Lord say, "His steadfast love endures forever."

Out of my distress I called on the Lord; the Lord answered me and set me in a broad place. With the Lord on my side I do not fear. What can mortals do to me? The Lord is on my side to help me; I shall look in triumph on those who hate me. It is better to take refuge in the Lord than to put confidence in mortals. It is better to take refuge in the Lord than to put confidence in princes.

All nations surrounded me; in the name of the Lord I cut them off! They surrounded me, surrounded me on every side; in the name of the Lord I cut them off! They surrounded me like bees; they blazed like a fire of thorns; in the name of the Lord I cut them off! I was pushed hard, so that I was falling, but the Lord helped me. The Lord is my strength and my might; he has become my salvation.

There are glad songs of victory in the tents of the righteous: "The right hand of the Lord does valiantly; the right hand of the Lord is exalted; the right hand of the Lord does valiantly." I shall not die, but I shall live, and recount the deeds of the Lord. The Lord has punished me severely, but he did not give me over to death. Open to me the gates of righteousness, that I may enter through them and give thanks to the Lord. This is the gate of the Lord; the righteous shall enter through it. I thank you that you have answered me and have become my salvation. The stone that the builders rejected has become the chief cornerstone. This is the Lord's doing; it is marvelous in our eyes. This is the day that the Lord has made; let us rejoice and be glad in it. Save us, we beseech you, O Lord! O Lord, we beseech you, give us success! Blessed is the one who comes in the name of the Lord. We bless you from the house of the Lord. The Lord is God, and he has given us light. Bind the festal procession with branches, up to the horns of the altar.

You are my God, and I will give thanks to you; you are my God, I will extol you. O give thanks to the Lord, for he is good, for his steadfast love endures forever.

Reflection:

Psalm 118 is a joyful psalm of thanksgiving and victory, celebrating God's steadfast love, salvation, and strength. The psalmist repeatedly emphasizes God's enduring love and invites all of Israel to proclaim it. From recounting personal deliverance from distress to declaring victory over adversity, the psalmist attributes everything to God's faithful love and mighty help. This psalm is a reminder to place our confidence in God rather than in human strength, rejoicing in His goodness, and giving thanks for His unchanging love.

1. The Enduring Love of the Lord (Verses 1-4)

The psalm begins with a powerful refrain: "His steadfast love endures forever." The psalmist invites Israel, the priests, and all who fear the Lord to declare this truth. This repeated statement serves as a grounding assurance, emphasizing God's unchanging love as the foundation of faith and gratitude. Reflect on how God's enduring love has been a constant in your life. Consider how His love serves as an anchor, regardless of circumstances.

Related Verse: Lamentations 3:22-23 – "The steadfast love of the Lord never ceases; his mercies never come to an end; they are new every morning; great is your faithfulness."

2. Trusting in God Over Human Power (Verses 5-9)

The psalmist recounts how, in times of distress, he called upon the Lord, who delivered him. The psalmist emphasizes that it is better to take refuge in the Lord than to trust in people, even in rulers. God's help provides true security, surpassing any human assistance or authority.

These verses challenge us to trust God above all else, placing our confidence in His unchanging character rather than relying solely on people or worldly systems.

Related Verse: Proverbs 3:5-6 – "Trust in the Lord with all your heart, and do not rely on your own insight. In all your ways acknowledge him, and he will make straight your paths."

3. God as Our Strength and Salvation (Verses 10-18)

Facing intense opposition, the psalmist declares that it is God's strength that has brought him victory. He celebrates with songs of deliverance and praises the "right hand of the Lord" for its mighty acts. The psalmist acknowledges that, although he faced hardship, God preserved him and did not abandon him to death.

These verses remind us that God is our strength and salvation in times of adversity, equipping us to endure challenges with confidence. Reflect on moments when God's strength sustained you, transforming hardship into victory.

Related Verse: Psalm 46:1 – "God is our refuge and strength, a very present help in trouble."

4. Rejoicing in God's Salvation and Goodness (Verses 19-29)

The psalmist concludes with gratitude, entering the "gates of righteousness" to praise the Lord. He celebrates the Lord's salvation, proclaiming, "The stone that the builders rejected has become the chief cornerstone," which foreshadows Christ as the foundation of salvation. The psalmist also declares, "This is the day that the Lord has made; let us rejoice and be glad in it." This passage calls us to rejoice in God's salvation and to see each day as a gift from Him. Reflect on how recognizing God's goodness and salvation can shape your daily outlook, leading you to live with gratitude and joy.

Related Verse: 1 Peter 2:6 – "For it stands in Scripture: 'See, I am laying in Zion a stone, a cornerstone chosen and precious; and whoever believes in him will not be put to shame.'"

Quote:
"God's love for us is as great as the strength of His hands, and His love endures as long as He endures." – Charles Spurgeon

Application:
This week, start each day by declaring God's steadfast love and reflecting on His faithfulness in your life. Place your confidence in God alone, acknowledging any areas where you may have relied too much on human support or resources. Let this confidence in God's strength lead you to celebrate His salvation and find joy in each day He has given.

Questions for Reflection:
- How has God's steadfast love been evident in my life?
- Are there areas where I need to place my trust in God over human strength?
- How can I rejoice in God's salvation and see each day as a gift?

Prayer:

Lord, thank You for Your steadfast love that endures forever. Help me to place my trust fully in You, knowing that You are my strength and my salvation. Teach me to rely on Your power rather than human strength and to live each day with gratitude and joy. Thank You for Your faithfulness, for being my cornerstone, and for the gift of salvation. Amen.

Memorization Guide:
Step 1: Break Down Key Sections

1. Verses 1-4: Proclaiming God's enduring love.
2. Verses 5-9: Trusting in God rather than human power.
3. Verses 10-18: Declaring God as our strength and salvation.
4. Verses 19-29: Rejoicing in God's salvation and goodness.

Step 2: Memorize by Key Themes and Visualizations

Section 1: God's Enduring Love (Verses 1-4)
- Picture yourself declaring God's steadfast love, finding joy in His unchanging nature.

Section 2: Trust in God Over People (Verses 5-9)
- Visualize placing your confidence in God's hands, above any human support.

Section 3: Strength and Salvation (Verses 10-18)
- Imagine God's powerful hand lifting you in times of trouble, bringing victory.

Section 4: Celebration of Salvation (Verses 19-29)
- Picture yourself entering God's "gates" with joy, grateful for each new day He has made.

Summary of Key Images
- Declaring and resting in God's steadfast love.
- Choosing trust in God over human strength.
- Experiencing God as our source of strength and salvation in adversity.
- Rejoicing in God's gift of each day and His eternal goodness.

Psalm 119:9-16: Living by God's Word
Psalm 119:9-16 (NRSV):

How can young people keep their way pure? By guarding it according to your word. With my whole heart I seek you; do not let me stray from your commandments. I treasure your word in my heart, so that I may not sin against you. Blessed are you, O Lord; teach me your statutes. With my lips I declare all the ordinances of your mouth. I delight in the way of your decrees as much as in all riches. I will meditate on your precepts, and fix my eyes on your ways. I will delight in your statutes; I will not forget your word.

Reflection:

This section of Psalm 119 speaks about the transformative power of God's Word, guiding us toward a life of purity and integrity. The psalmist emphasizes the importance of internalizing God's commandments, seeking Him wholeheartedly, and finding joy in His ways. These verses remind us that keeping God's Word close protects us from sin and strengthens our commitment to Him.

1. Guarding Our Way by God's Word (Verse 9)

The psalmist begins with a question: "How can young people keep their way pure?" The answer is clear—by living according to God's Word. This verse reminds us that Scripture is not just a guidebook but a protective shield, helping us navigate life's challenges while keeping our hearts and actions aligned with God's will.

Reflect on how applying God's Word in daily life can guard your heart and actions. Consider how His Word is a compass, helping you stay on the path He's set for you.

Related Verse: Proverbs 4:23 – "Keep your heart with all vigilance, for from it flow the springs of life."

2. Wholehearted Seeking and Treasuring God's Word (Verses 10-11)

The psalmist expresses a deep desire to seek God with his whole heart and to treasure God's Word in his heart. By storing up God's Word, the psalmist is empowered to resist sin and stay faithful. This wholehearted seeking reflects an intentional commitment to knowing God intimately and allowing His Word to take root in our lives.

These verses encourage us to seek God with sincerity and to let His Word dwell richly in us. Reflect on what it means to truly treasure God's Word and how that treasure can shape your daily choices.

Related Verse: Colossians 3:16 – "Let the word of Christ dwell in you richly; teach and admonish one another in all wisdom."

3. Declaring and Delighting in God's Decrees (Verses 12-14)

The psalmist moves from internalizing God's Word to expressing it outwardly, declaring God's statutes and finding joy in His decrees. He values God's commands "as much as in all riches," showing that he treasures God's wisdom above material wealth. This delight in God's ways reflects a heart that finds fulfillment in obedience and reverence.

These verses challenge us to see God's commandments as a source of joy and fulfillment, not as burdensome rules. Reflect on how declaring God's Word with joy can deepen your appreciation for His wisdom and guidance.

Related Verse: Jeremiah 15:16 – "Your words were found, and I ate them, and your words became to me a joy and the delight of my heart."

4. Meditating on God's Precepts and Fixing Our Eyes on His Ways

(Verses 15-16)

The psalmist concludes this passage by committing to meditate on God's precepts and to fix his eyes on His ways. Meditating on God's Word helps us understand His heart, and keeping our focus on His ways strengthens our walk. This dedication to not forgetting God's Word reflects a sincere devotion to living a life that honors Him.

These final verses remind us that sustained focus on God's Word keeps us aligned with His will. Reflect on how making space to meditate on Scripture and keeping your focus on God's truth can bring you greater clarity and peace.

Related Verse: Joshua 1:8 – "This book of the law shall not depart out of your mouth; you shall meditate on it day and night, so that you may be careful to act in accordance with all that is written in it."

Quote:

"The Bible will keep you from sin, or sin will keep you from the Bible." – D.L. Moody

---

Application:

This week, set aside time to memorize and meditate on a specific verse or passage that speaks to you. Let God's Word dwell richly in your heart, becoming a source of strength and guidance. Consider ways to actively declare and share His truth with others, allowing God's wisdom to shine through your words and actions. Make it your goal to treasure God's Word and keep it close as a foundation for your daily choices.

Questions for Reflection:

- How can I allow God's Word to shape and protect my heart?

- What specific steps can I take to treasure God's Word more deeply?
- How can I find joy and fulfillment in God's commandments?

Prayer:
Lord, thank You for Your Word, which is a light to my path and a shield to my heart. Help me to seek You wholeheartedly and to treasure Your Word deeply. Give me the desire to meditate on Your precepts and to declare Your truth with joy. May Your Word dwell richly in my heart, guiding me and protecting me each day. Amen.

Memorization Guide:
Step 1: Break Down Key Sections
1. Verse 9: Guarding our way by God's Word.
2. Verses 10-11: Wholeheartedly seeking and treasuring God's Word.
3. Verses 12-14: Declaring and delighting in God's decrees.
4. Verses 15-16: Meditating on God's precepts and keeping our focus on His ways.

Step 2: Memorize by Key Themes and Visualizations
Section 1: Guarding by God's Word (Verse 9)
- Visualize God's Word as a protective shield, guiding your steps.

Section 2: Wholehearted Seeking (Verses 10-11)
- Picture yourself holding God's Word as a precious treasure, close to your heart.

Section 3: Declaring and Delighting (Verses 12-14)
- Imagine speaking God's Word with joy, sharing it as a source of true wealth.

Section 4: Meditating and Focusing (Verses 15-16)
- Visualize fixing your eyes on God's Word, letting it fill your mind and guide your heart.

Summary of Key Images
- God's Word as a guide and protector of our way.
- Treasuring God's Word with a sincere, wholehearted commitment.
- Declaring and finding joy in God's commandments.
- Meditating on and focusing on God's precepts to stay aligned with His truth.

Psalm 121: The Lord Is Your Keeper
Psalm 121 (NRSV):

I lift up my eyes to the hills—from where will my help come? My help comes from the Lord, who made heaven and earth. He will not let your foot be moved; he who keeps you will not slumber. He who keeps Israel will neither slumber nor sleep.

The Lord is your keeper; the Lord is your shade at your right hand. The sun shall not strike you by day, nor the moon by night. The Lord will keep you from all evil; he will keep your life. The Lord will keep your going out and your coming in from this time on and forevermore.

Reflection:

Psalm 121 is a comforting psalm that affirms God as our ever-watchful keeper and protector. It opens with the psalmist looking toward the hills and asking, "From where will my help come?" His answer is immediate and confident: "My help comes from the Lord." This psalm highlights God's constant care, emphasizing that He never sleeps and is always present to protect His people from harm, day and night. Through the imagery of God as a shade and keeper, Psalm 121 assures us that He guards every aspect of our lives, from our daily activities to our future.

1. Looking to God for Help (Verses 1-2)

The psalmist begins by lifting his eyes to the hills, a symbol of strength and refuge, and asking where his help will come from. The answer is that his help comes from the Creator of all—the One who made heaven and earth. This opening verse invites us to remember that our help is not found in earthly places but in the Lord, who has power over all creation.

Reflect on where you turn when you need help. Consider how

trusting in God, the Maker of heaven and earth, offers a foundation of hope and strength beyond any worldly resource.
Related Verse: Isaiah 40:28 – "Have you not known? Have you not heard? The Lord is the everlasting God, the Creator of the ends of the earth. He does not faint or grow weary; his understanding is unsearchable."

2. God's Unfailing Vigilance (Verses 3-4)

The psalmist assures us that God will not let our "foot be moved" and that He "will not slumber." Unlike humans who need rest, God is tireless and always vigilant. His constant watch over His people, both individually and collectively, means that we can rest knowing He is awake and aware of every detail of our lives. These verses encourage us to find peace in God's constant presence, knowing He is never inattentive or unaware of our needs. Reflect on the comfort of God's unwavering attention and His tireless care for you.
Related Verse: Psalm 34:15 – "The eyes of the Lord are on the righteous, and his ears are open to their cry."

3. Protection Day and Night (Verses 5-6)

The psalmist describes the Lord as a shade at our right hand, protecting us from both the sun by day and the moon by night. This imagery of God as a shade implies close, personal protection, sheltering us from the scorching heat and the darkness. God's protection covers every moment of our day, both seen and unseen, physical and spiritual.

This passage reminds us that God is present in every aspect of our lives, guarding us continuously. Reflect on how His protection encompasses all times and places, providing a refuge no matter what we face.
Related Verse: Psalm 91:1 – "Whoever dwells in the shelter of the

Most High will rest in the shadow of the Almighty."

4. The Lord's Lifelong Keeping (Verses 7-8)

The psalm concludes with a promise that God will keep us from all evil and will preserve our life. God's keeping extends to our "going out and coming in," a phrase that symbolizes the entirety of life's journey. His protection is not temporary but endures "from this time on and forevermore," assuring us that He will guard our path in all circumstances and all seasons.

These final verses encourage us to rest in God's eternal keeping, knowing that He cares for us at every stage of life. Reflect on the assurance that God's love and protection are constant, even in times of uncertainty or change.

Related Verse: Deuteronomy 31:8 – "It is the Lord who goes before you. He will be with you; he will not fail you or forsake you. Do not fear or be dismayed."

Quote:

"God's care is more constant and certain than the rising of the sun and moon, guarding us in every season." – Charles Spurgeon

Application:

This week, focus on placing your trust in God's constant care. When you feel uncertain or worried, lift your eyes and remind yourself of God's unfailing protection. Take time to pray over specific areas of your life, entrusting them to God's keeping. Rest in the assurance that He is present, protecting you at all times and in every circumstance, both now and forever.

Questions for Reflection:

- Where do I turn for help when I feel anxious or in need?

- How does knowing that God is constantly vigilant over me bring me comfort?
- In what areas of my life can I more fully trust God's keeping and protection?

Prayer:
Lord, thank You for being my keeper, my ever-present help. I lift my eyes to You, knowing that You watch over me tirelessly. Help me to trust in Your constant care and to rest in Your protection. Thank You for guarding my life, my coming and going, today and forevermore. Amen.

Memorization Guide:
Step 1: Break Down Key Sections
1. Verses 1-2: Looking to God as our ultimate source of help.
2. Verses 3-4: Finding peace in God's unwavering vigilance.
3. Verses 5-6: Trusting in God's protection day and night.
4. Verses 7-8: Resting in God's lifelong care and keeping.

Step 2: Memorize by Key Themes and Visualizations
Section 1: God as Our Help (Verses 1-2)
- Visualize lifting your eyes toward the hills, seeking strength from the Creator.

Section 2: God's Constant Watch (Verses 3-4)
- Picture God as an ever-watchful guardian, awake and attentive to your needs.

Section 3: Day and Night Protection (Verses 5-6)
- Imagine God's shade covering you, providing protection and peace from every threat.

Section 4: Lifelong Keeping (Verses 7-8)

- Visualize God's hand guiding you on every path, securing your steps at every turn.

Summary of Key Images
- Looking to God as our ultimate help and source of strength.
- Resting in God's vigilant watch, knowing He never slumbers.
- Experiencing God's protection as a constant shade, day and night.
- Finding peace in God's lifelong keeping, encompassing every aspect of our journey.

Psalm 130: Waiting on the Lord with Hope

Psalm 130 (NRSV):

Out of the depths I cry to you, O Lord. Lord, hear my voice! Let your ears be attentive to the voice of my supplications! If you, O Lord, should mark iniquities, Lord, who could stand? But there is forgiveness with you, so that you may be revered.

I wait for the Lord, my soul waits, and in his word I hope; my soul waits for the Lord more than those who watch for the morning, more than those who watch for the morning. O Israel, hope in the Lord! For with the Lord there is steadfast love, and with him is great power to redeem. It is he who will redeem Israel from all its iniquities.

Reflection:

Psalm 130 is a profound prayer of repentance, trust, and hope. It begins with the psalmist crying out "from the depths," a phrase that signifies despair or deep distress, yet the tone quickly turns toward hope and trust in God's mercy and forgiveness. This psalm reflects the tension of waiting for God while resting in the assurance of His unfailing love and redemptive power.

1. Crying Out from the Depths (Verses 1-2)

The psalmist begins by crying out to God "from the depths," a place of desperation and need. He pleads for God to hear his supplications, expressing vulnerability and a desire for God's attentive mercy. This section reminds us that God is a refuge we can turn to, especially in times of anguish or guilt.

Reflect on times when you have felt "in the depths" and consider how God has responded to your cries. Trust that He is attentive and compassionate, always ready to listen.

Related Verse: Psalm 34:17 – "When the righteous cry for help, the Lord hears, and rescues them from all their troubles."

---

2. Acknowledging God's Forgiveness (Verses 3-4)

The psalmist acknowledges that no one could stand if God kept a record of sins, but then rejoices in the forgiveness God offers. This forgiveness is not only a source of freedom from guilt but inspires reverence and awe for God. The psalmist's understanding of God's mercy becomes a foundation for his faith and worship.

These verses remind us that God's forgiveness is a gift that draws us closer to Him, freeing us from guilt and inviting us into a deeper relationship. Reflect on how God's forgiveness has brought you peace and encouraged you to revere Him.

Related Verse: 1 John 1:9 – "If we confess our sins, he who is faithful and just will forgive us our sins and cleanse us from all unrighteousness."

3. Waiting with Hope in God's Word (Verses 5-6)

The psalmist expresses a deep trust in God's promises, waiting on the Lord with expectant hope. He likens this anticipation to those who watch for the morning, emphasizing a sense of certainty and eagerness. In God's word, the psalmist finds a steadfast hope that sustains him during his waiting.

These verses encourage us to patiently wait on God, trusting that His promises will be fulfilled. Reflect on how placing hope in God's word can bring peace and strength in seasons of waiting.

Related Verse: Isaiah 40:31 – "But those who wait for the Lord shall renew their strength, they shall mount up with wings like eagles, they shall run and not be weary, they shall walk and not faint."

4. Assurance of Redemption and Steadfast Love (Verses 7-8)

The psalm concludes with a call to hope, declaring that God's love is steadfast and His power to redeem is great. The psalmist assures Israel of God's redemption from sin, highlighting that God's compassion and strength bring freedom and restoration. This final declaration calls us to find confidence in God's enduring love and His ability to redeem even the darkest situations.

These verses invite us to trust in God's redemptive power and steadfast love, knowing He is always at work in our lives. Reflect on areas where you need redemption and rest in the assurance that God's love and power are sufficient to restore and renew.

Related Verse: Titus 2:14 – "He it is who gave himself for us that he might redeem us from all iniquity and purify for himself a people of his own who are zealous for good deeds."

Quote:

"To wait on God is to find our strength renewed, our hope assured, and our hearts aligned with His purpose." – A.W. Tozer

Application:

This week, take time to meditate on God's forgiveness and the hope found in His word. When you feel anxious or in need of answers, turn to God in prayer, expressing your trust in His timing. Let this season of waiting draw you closer to God, allowing His word to strengthen your hope. Remember that His steadfast love and redemptive power are at work in your life, even when answers feel distant.

Questions for Reflection:

- How have I experienced God's forgiveness, and how does it inspire me to draw closer to Him?

- What does it look like to wait on God with hope and trust in His promises?

- Are there areas in my life where I need God's redemption and renewal?

Prayer:
Lord, thank You for hearing my cries and for the gift of Your forgiveness. Help me to wait on You with hope, trusting in Your promises and timing. Strengthen my heart to rest in Your steadfast love and to hold fast to Your word. Redeem and renew me, and may my life reflect the hope and peace that come from trusting in You. Amen.

Memorization Guide:
Step 1: Break Down Key Sections
1. Verses 1-2: Crying out to God from the depths.
2. Verses 3-4: Acknowledging God's forgiveness and revering Him.
3. Verses 5-6: Waiting with hope in God's word.
4. Verses 7-8: Assurance of God's steadfast love and redemption.

Step 2: Memorize by Key Themes and Visualizations
Section 1: Crying Out (Verses 1-2)
- Visualize reaching out to God, calling on Him from a place of need and distress.

Section 2: Forgiveness and Reverence (Verses 3-4)
- Picture God's forgiveness washing over you, bringing peace and reverence.

Section 3: Waiting with Hope (Verses 5-6)

- Imagine yourself waiting with anticipation, like watching for dawn, grounded in God's word.

Section 4: Redemption and Love (Verses 7-8)
- Picture God's love and redemptive power covering you, bringing restoration and hope.

Summary of Key Images

- Crying out to God in times of deep need and distress.
- Finding peace and reverence in God's forgiveness.
- Waiting on God with hope, trusting in His promises.
- Resting in God's steadfast love and redemptive power for renewal.

Psalm 138: Gratitude and Confidence in God's Faithfulness
Psalm 138 (NRSV):

I give you thanks, O Lord, with my whole heart; before the gods I sing your praise; I bow down toward your holy temple and give thanks to your name for your steadfast love and your faithfulness; for you have exalted your name and your word above everything. On the day I called, you answered me, you increased my strength of soul.

All the kings of the earth shall praise you, O Lord, for they have heard the words of your mouth. They shall sing of the ways of the Lord, for great is the glory of the Lord. For though the Lord is high, he regards the lowly; but the haughty he perceives from far away.

Though I walk in the midst of trouble, you preserve me against the wrath of my enemies; you stretch out your hand, and your right hand delivers me. The Lord will fulfill his purpose for me; your steadfast love, O Lord, endures forever. Do not forsake the work of your hands.

Reflection:

Psalm 138 is a heartfelt expression of gratitude, confidence, and trust in God's faithfulness. The psalmist opens with thanksgiving, praising God's steadfast love and responsiveness. The psalm moves from personal gratitude to a broader vision of all people honoring God and concludes with an affirmation of trust that God will fulfill His purposes. It reminds us that God is exalted yet intimately involved in our lives, strengthening us in times of trouble and guiding us in His unfailing love.

1. Wholehearted Thanksgiving for God's Love and Faithfulness (Verses 1-2)

The psalmist begins with a declaration of thanks, "with my whole heart," for God's steadfast love and faithfulness. He acknowledges that God has "exalted" His name and His word, holding them as the foundation for all that is good and true. The psalmist's gratitude flows from God's reliable character, which sustains and strengthens him.

These verses invite us to approach God with wholehearted thanksgiving, acknowledging His love and faithfulness. Reflect on how God's word and presence have been a source of strength in your life, and let this lead you to deeper gratitude.

Related Verse: Psalm 100:4 – "Enter his gates with thanksgiving, and his courts with praise; give thanks to him, bless his name."

2. Declaring God's Glory to All (Verses 3-5)

The psalmist speaks of how God responded to him in times of need, increasing his "strength of soul." This experience of God's faithfulness leads him to envision all people, including rulers, praising God for His glory and His ways. The psalmist emphasizes that God's greatness and glory are evident to all who are willing to listen.

These verses encourage us to share God's faithfulness and glory with others, declaring His greatness. Reflect on how you can share God's goodness with those around you, pointing them toward His love and power.

Related Verse: Isaiah 12:4 – "Give thanks to the Lord, call on his name; make known his deeds among the nations; proclaim that his name is exalted."

3. God's Care in Times of Trouble (Verse 7)

The psalmist acknowledges God's protection even "in the midst of trouble." Despite challenges, he trusts that God will preserve him, delivering him from harm with His powerful "right hand." This verse reminds us of God's presence and help, even in our darkest times, protecting and sustaining us.

These words offer comfort, encouraging us to trust in God's protection. Reflect on times when God has preserved you, and remember that His hand is still there, ready to guide and shield you.

Related Verse: Psalm 46:1 – "God is our refuge and strength, a very present help in trouble."

---

4. Trusting God's Purpose and Enduring Love (Verse 8)

The psalmist concludes with a confident declaration that "The Lord will fulfill his purpose for me." He rests in God's steadfast love, assured that God will not abandon "the work of [His] hands." This final affirmation is a statement of trust in God's ongoing work in our lives, knowing He is faithful to complete what He has started.

These verses remind us that God has a purpose for each of us, and His love is unchanging. Reflect on how trusting God's purpose can bring peace, even when you cannot see the full picture.

Related Verse: Philippians 1:6 – "I am confident of this, that the one who began a good work among you will bring it to completion by the day of Jesus Christ."

Quote:
"God's faithfulness is not dependent on our faithfulness. His promises stand firm because He is unchanging." – A.W. Tozer

---

Application:
This week, begin each day by giving thanks to God for His love and faithfulness. Reflect on specific ways He has answered prayers, strengthened you, and shown His presence in your life.

Look for opportunities to share a testimony of God's faithfulness with others, reminding them of His goodness. Trust in God's ongoing work in your life, resting in His promise to fulfill His purpose for you.

Questions for Reflection:
- How has God shown His steadfast love and faithfulness in my life recently?
- In what ways can I declare God's greatness to those around me?
- Do I trust that God will fulfill His purpose for me, even in times of difficulty?

Prayer:

Lord, thank You for Your unfailing love and faithfulness. I praise You with my whole heart, grateful for Your steadfast presence in my life. Help me to trust in Your purpose, even in challenging times. Give me the courage to share Your goodness with others and to rest in Your promise to complete the work You have begun in me. Amen.

Memorization Guide:

Step 1: Break Down Key Sections
1. Verses 1-2: Wholehearted thanksgiving for God's steadfast love and faithfulness.
2. Verses 3-5: Declaring God's glory to all people.
3. Verse 7: Trusting in God's protection and presence in times of trouble.
4. Verse 8: Confidence in God's purpose and enduring love.

Step 2: Memorize by Key Themes and Visualizations

Section 1: Thanksgiving (Verses 1-2)
- Picture bowing down in gratitude, giving thanks for God's steadfast love.

Section 2: Declaring God's Glory (Verses 3-5)
- Imagine sharing God's greatness with others, letting His love shine through.

Section 3: God's Protection (Verse 7)
- Visualize God's hand shielding you, preserving you in times of trouble.

Section 4: Trust in God's Purpose (Verse 8)
- Picture resting peacefully in God's promise to complete His work in you.

Summary of Key Images
- Wholehearted thanksgiving for God's love and faithfulness.
- Sharing God's glory with others, inviting all to praise Him.
- Trusting in God's protection in the midst of trouble.
- Confidently resting in God's purpose, trusting His love to endure.

Psalm 139: Known and Loved by God

Psalm 139 (NRSV):

O Lord, you have searched me and known me. You know when I sit down and when I rise up; you discern my thoughts from far away. You search out my path and my lying down, and are acquainted with all my ways. Even before a word is on my tongue, O Lord, you know it completely. You hem me in, behind and before, and lay your hand upon me. Such knowledge is too wonderful for me; it is so high that I cannot attain it.

Where can I go from your spirit? Or where can I flee from your presence? If I ascend to heaven, you are there; if I make my bed in Sheol, you are there. If I take the wings of the morning and settle at the farthest limits of the sea, even there your hand shall lead me, and your right hand shall hold me fast. If I say, "Surely the darkness shall cover me, and the light around me become night," even the darkness is not dark to you; the night is as bright as the day, for darkness is as light to you.

For it was you who formed my inward parts; you knit me together in my mother's womb. I praise you, for I am fearfully and wonderfully made. Wonderful are your works; that I know very well. My frame was not hidden from you, when I was being made in secret, intricately woven in the depths of the earth. Your eyes beheld my unformed substance. In your book were written all the days that were formed for me, when none of them as yet existed.

How weighty to me are your thoughts, O God! How vast is the sum of them! I try to count them—they are more than the sand; I come to the end—I am still with you.

O that you would kill the wicked, O God, and that the bloodthirsty would depart from me—those who speak of you maliciously, and lift themselves up against you for evil! Do I not hate those who hate you, O Lord? And do I not loathe those who rise up against you? I hate them with perfect hatred; I count them my enemies.

Search me, O God, and know my heart; test me and know my thoughts. See if there is any wicked way in me, and lead me in the way everlasting.

Reflection:

Psalm 139 is a beautiful meditation on God's intimate knowledge and presence. The psalmist reflects on God's profound understanding of every detail of our lives, from our thoughts to our paths, declaring that God's knowledge of us is "too wonderful." This psalm expresses a deep sense of being known and loved by God, who is present in every moment and place, from the heights of heaven to the depths of the earth. It ends with an invitation for God to search our hearts and guide us in the way everlasting.

1. God's Intimate Knowledge (Verses 1-6)

The psalm opens with a declaration that God has "searched" and "known" us. Every detail of our lives, our thoughts, actions, and words, is fully known by God. This knowledge is described as "wonderful"—beyond our understanding but profoundly comforting.

These verses remind us that we are never unknown or unseen by God. Reflect on the comfort that comes from being fully known and loved, knowing that God cares deeply for every aspect of your life.

Related Verse: Jeremiah 1:5 – "Before I formed you in the womb I knew you, and before you were born I consecrated you."

---

2. God's Unescapable Presence (Verses 7-12)

The psalmist marvels that there is nowhere we can go to escape God's presence. Whether in the heights of heaven, the depths of Sheol, or the farthest reaches of the sea, God is there, guiding us and holding us fast. Even darkness cannot hide us from God, for "the night is as bright as the day" to Him.

These verses encourage us to trust in God's unceasing presence, especially when we feel alone or distant from Him. Reflect on how knowing God is always with you can provide peace and assurance in every situation.

Related Verse: Romans 8:38-39 – "For I am convinced that neither death, nor life, nor angels, nor rulers, nor things present, nor things to come…will be able to separate us from the love of God in Christ Jesus our Lord."

3. Wonderfully Made by God (Verses 13-16)

The psalmist celebrates God's creative power, acknowledging that He formed our "inward parts" and "knit us together" in the womb. Each of us is "fearfully and wonderfully made," and God has ordained our days before we even existed. This section reveals God's intentionality and care in creating each of us uniquely.

These verses remind us of our value and purpose, created intentionally by God. Reflect on how being "wonderfully made" by God can shape your self-worth and help you embrace your purpose in life.

Related Verse: Ephesians 2:10 – "For we are his workmanship, created in Christ Jesus for good works, which God prepared beforehand, that we should walk in them."

4. Invitation for God to Search Our Hearts (Verses 17-24)

The psalmist ends by inviting God to "search me, O God, and

know my heart." He asks God to reveal any "wicked way" within him and to lead him in the way everlasting. This humble request shows a desire for purity and a life aligned with God's ways, open to God's guidance and correction.

These verses encourage us to invite God into our hearts, allowing Him to reveal areas that need growth. Reflect on how opening your heart to God's guidance can lead you toward a life of integrity and purpose.

Related Verse: Psalm 51:10 – "Create in me a clean heart, O God, and renew a right spirit within me."

Quote:

"To be loved but not known is superficial. To be known but not loved is painful. But to be fully known and truly loved by God is freeing beyond measure." – Timothy Keller

Application:

This week, reflect on the comfort of being fully known and loved by God. Take time to meditate on the truth that God is always with you and has purposefully created you with love. Ask God to search your heart, revealing anything that needs healing or growth. Trust that His presence is constant, even in life's darkest or most uncertain moments, and let His knowledge and care guide you.

Questions for Reflection:

- How does knowing that God fully knows and loves me change my perspective on life's challenges?
- In what ways do I experience God's presence, especially in difficult times?

- Am I willing to invite God to search my heart and guide me toward growth?

Prayer:

Lord, thank You for knowing me completely and for Your unchanging presence in my life. I am grateful to be fearfully and wonderfully made by You. Search my heart, Lord, and guide me in the way everlasting. Help me to walk in the confidence of Your love and to trust that You are with me in every moment. Amen.

Memorization Guide:

Step 1: Break Down Key Sections

1. Verses 1-6: God's intimate knowledge of us.
2. Verses 7-12: God's unescapable presence.
3. Verses 13-16: Celebrating being wonderfully made by God.
4. Verses 17-24: Invitation for God to search and guide our hearts.

Step 2: Memorize by Key Themes and Visualizations

Section 1: God's Knowledge (Verses 1-6)

- Picture God knowing every detail of your life, understanding your heart and mind fully.

Section 2: Unescapable Presence (Verses 7-12)

- Visualize God's presence in every corner of your life, even in the darkest places.

Section 3: Wonderfully Made (Verses 13-16)

- Imagine God carefully and lovingly forming you, affirming your worth and purpose.

Section 4: Invitation to Search (Verses 17-24)

- Picture opening your heart to God, welcoming His guidance and seeking a pure path.

Summary of Key Images

- God's intimate knowledge of every thought, action, and word.
- God's unchanging presence that follows us everywhere.
- The wonder of being purposefully and lovingly created by God.
- The invitation to God to search our hearts and guide us.

Psalm 145: Celebrating God's Greatness and Compassion

Psalm 145 (NRSV):

I will extol you, my God and King, and bless your name forever and ever. Every day I will bless you, and praise your name forever and ever. Great is the Lord, and greatly to be praised; his greatness is unsearchable.

One generation shall laud your works to another, and shall declare your mighty acts. On the glorious splendor of your majesty, and on your wondrous works, I will meditate. The might of your awesome deeds shall be proclaimed, and I will declare your greatness. They shall celebrate the fame of your abundant goodness, and shall sing aloud of your righteousness.

The Lord is gracious and merciful, slow to anger and abounding in steadfast love. The Lord is good to all, and his compassion is over all that he has made. All your works shall give thanks to you, O Lord, and all your faithful shall bless you. They shall speak of the glory of your kingdom, and tell of your power, to make known to all people your mighty deeds, and the glorious splendor of your kingdom. Your kingdom is an everlasting kingdom, and your dominion endures throughout all generations.

The Lord is faithful in all his words, and gracious in all his deeds. The Lord upholds all who are falling, and raises up all who are bowed down. The eyes of all look to you, and you give them their food in due season. You open your hand, satisfying the desire of every living thing.

The Lord is just in all his ways, and kind in all his doings. The Lord is near to all who call on him, to all who call on him in truth. He fulfills the desire of all who fear him; he also hears their cry, and saves them. The Lord watches over all who love him, but all the wicked he will destroy.

My mouth will speak the praise of the Lord, and all flesh will bless his holy name forever and ever.

Reflection:

Psalm 145 is a majestic declaration of praise, capturing the vastness of God's greatness, the enduring nature of His kingdom, and His compassionate care for all creation. The psalmist begins by extolling God daily and meditates on God's splendor and mighty works, inviting all generations to know and celebrate His abundant goodness. Psalm 145 emphasizes God's mercy, His provision, and His faithfulness to those who seek Him, creating a beautiful picture of a loving and powerful King.

1. Praising God's Unsearchable Greatness (Verses 1-3)

The psalm opens with a commitment to bless God's name every day and to praise His unsearchable greatness. The psalmist recognizes that God's majesty is beyond human understanding, inspiring awe and reverence.

Reflect on God's greatness in your life, and consider how you can cultivate a daily rhythm of praising Him. Let your praise be a response to His boundless power and grace.

Related Verse: Psalm 96:4 – "For great is the Lord, and greatly to be praised; he is to be feared above all gods."

2. Passing Down God's Works to Future Generations (Verses 4-7)

The psalmist celebrates how one generation shall declare God's works to another, creating a legacy of worship and reverence. Meditating on God's splendor and proclaiming His greatness allows us to inspire faith in future generations.

Reflect on how you can share God's goodness with others, passing down stories of His faithfulness and provision. Consider the power of testimony in encouraging others in their walk with God.

Related Verse: Deuteronomy 6:6-7 – "Keep these words that I am commanding you today in your heart. Recite them to your children and talk about them when you are at home and when you are away."

---

3. God's Compassion and Steadfast Love (Verses 8-13)

These verses describe God's gracious and merciful nature, highlighting His compassion for all He has created. The psalmist celebrates God's kindness, declaring that His kingdom endures forever. God's love is evident not only in His power but also in His gentle care for each of us.

These verses invite us to reflect on God's compassion in our lives, reminding us that His kindness is constant and enduring. Take time to appreciate God's patience and love, especially in moments of weakness.

Related Verse: Exodus 34:6 – "The Lord, the Lord, a God merciful and gracious, slow to anger, and abounding in steadfast love and faithfulness."

---

4. God's Provision and Faithfulness (Verses 14-16)

The psalmist acknowledges that God upholds those who are falling and provides for all living things. God opens His hand and satisfies the desires of every creature, faithfully caring for all of His creation.

These verses remind us to trust in God's provision, knowing that He is attentive to our needs. Reflect on how God has provided for you in every season, and allow this assurance to strengthen your trust in His care.

Related Verse: Philippians 4:19 – "And my God will fully satisfy every need of yours according to his riches in glory in Christ Jesus."

5. God's Nearness and Justice (Verses 17-21)

The psalm concludes by celebrating God's justice, kindness, and nearness to those who call on Him. The psalmist assures us that God hears the cries of those who fear Him and protects those who love Him. This nearness is a source of comfort and encouragement, knowing that God is ever-present and attentive.

These final verses invite us to draw near to God in truth, confident that He hears and cares for us. Reflect on the peace that comes from knowing that God watches over you and desires a close relationship with you.

Related Verse: James 4:8 – "Draw near to God, and he will draw near to you."

Quote:

"The heart of God is revealed in His kindness, patience, and nearness to those who seek Him with a humble heart." – Charles Spurgeon

---

Application:

This week, take time each day to praise God for His greatness and goodness. Reflect on specific ways He has shown you kindness, compassion, and provision. Share a story of God's faithfulness with someone else, whether through a conversation, a letter, or social media, as a testimony of His love. Let this psalm inspire you to draw closer to God, trusting in His unfailing care and celebrating His unsearchable greatness.

Questions for Reflection:

- How can I cultivate a daily practice of praising God's greatness?
- In what ways has God shown me compassion and provided for me?
- How can I share stories of God's faithfulness with others, creating a legacy of praise?

Prayer:

Lord, I praise You for Your greatness and for Your abundant goodness. Thank You for being gracious and compassionate, always providing and upholding me. Help me to share Your love with others, proclaiming Your mighty works and trusting in Your faithfulness. May my life be a testimony of Your steadfast love, inspiring others to seek and honor You. Amen.

Memorization Guide:

Step 1: Break Down Key Sections

1. Verses 1-3: Daily praise for God's unsearchable greatness.
2. Verses 4-7: Passing down stories of God's works and faithfulness.
3. Verses 8-13: Celebrating God's compassion, kindness, and eternal kingdom.
4. Verses 14-16: Trusting in God's provision and care.
5. Verses 17-21: Drawing near to God, confident in His justice and protection.

Step 2: Memorize by Key Themes and Visualizations

Section 1: God's Greatness (Verses 1-3)

- Picture yourself offering daily praise, captivated by God's unsearchable power.

Section 2: Passing Down God's Works (Verses 4-7)

- Visualize sharing stories of God's goodness, inspiring others to worship Him.

Section 3: God's Compassion (Verses 8-13)

- Imagine God's love as a gentle and constant presence, offering compassion and mercy.

Section 4: Provision and Faithfulness (Verses 14-16)

- Picture God's hand reaching out, providing for and sustaining all of creation.

Section 5: Nearness and Justice (Verses 17-21)

- Visualize God's presence close beside you, listening and protecting with care.

Summary of Key Images

- Daily praise for God's unsearchable greatness and power.
- Passing down a legacy of worship, sharing God's works across generations.
- Celebrating God's compassion, kindness, and eternal kingdom.
- Trusting in God's faithful provision for all creation.
- Drawing near to God, confident in His justice and constant protection.

The Author

My name is Jeff Crosby, and I am a Christian. I am a husband and a father. I am a former pastor. I am a US Army combat veteran. I served two tours in Iraq. The Psalms have always been a huge help to me in my own struggle with mental health as well as in the circumstances I've faced in this life. Without the love and peace of Christ I wouldn't be here today. Thank you to everyone who has invested in me, who has spoken life to me, who has mentored and encouraged me over the years.

Made in the USA
Middletown, DE
07 February 2025